HOW LIBERALS ARE
WRECKING
THE AMERICAN ECONOMY

& WHAT YOU CAN DO TO PROTECT YOURSELF

How Liberals Are Wrecking The American Economy
& What You Can Do To Protect Yourself

Copyright © 2016, by James R. Cook

All rights reserved.

Published by:

Investment Rarities Incorporated

7850 Metro Parkway
Minneapolis, Minnesota 55425
1-800-328-1860
www.investmentrarities.com

Please contact the publisher for additional copies.

TABLE OF CONTENTS:

Chapter 1 Blameless .... Page 5
Chapter 2 The Road to Perdition .... Page 8
Chapter 3 Destroying Wealth .... Page 10
Chapter 4 Destroying Western Civilization .... Page 13
Chapter 5 National Suicide .... Page 17
Chapter 6 The Economics of Armageddon .... Page 20
Chapter 7 Truth Teller .... Page 23
Chapter 8 Air War .... Page 27
Chapter 9 Job Creation .... Page 29
Chapter 10 Nauseating .... Page 31
Chapter 11 What Liberals Can't Comprehend .... Page 33
Chapter 12 The Economist Who Saw the Future .... Page 36
Chapter 13 House of Cards .... Page 38
Chapter 14 A Little Paranoia is Good .... Page 41
Chapter 15 The Approaching Calamity .... Page 44
Chapter 16 Bread and Circuses .... Page 48
Chapter 17 Parents of the Year .... Page 50
Chapter 18 Liberal Envy .... Page 53
Chapter 19 Expropriate the Capitalists .... Page 55
Chapter 20 Ignoring Risk .... Page 58
Chapter 21 Without Merit .... Page 61
Chapter 22 The Keynesian Fallacy .... Page 64
Chapter 23 The Enemy Within .... Page 68
Chapter 24 Egalitarian Nonsense .... Page 70
Chapter 25 Food for Thought .... Page 74
Chapter 26 What You Should Do Now .... Page 76

INTRODUCTION

For the past few decades economic policies advocated by the left have prevailed in our country. The Federal Reserve and the Treasury are run by liberals who practice Keynesian monetary expansion. Our liberal government runs huge spending deficits and the Federal Reserve provides the Treasury with newly created money to pay the government's bills. This is a form of currency debasement that reduces the purchasing power of the dollar.

Progressive programs like quantitative easing create new money that causes asset inflation. The owners of stocks, bonds, farmland, art and antiques see enormous appreciation. Meanwhile, the middle class who own none of these assets see their cost of living rise. Income inequality is caused by liberal policies. Artificially low interest rates promoted by liberals deprive savers and retirees of income. The liberal agenda hurts working people.

High tax policies, regulations that promote progressive fads, welfare programs, government subsidies, and excessive litigation have hurt the economy. Our inability to break free of the great recession and get our economy back on track comes from these liberal programs. In time they will sink us and cause great economic hardship. The liberal agenda is the blueprint for national ruin.

The government, Wall Street and the media tell us that all is well. This book seeks to disprove that contention. Don't believe them. Liberal policies are ruining America and we are going to suffer for it.

James R. Cook

CHAPTER 1

BLAMELESS

"Modern capitalism benefited the masses in a double way – both by greatly increasing the wages of the masses of workers and greatly reducing the real prices they had to pay for what was produced." **Henry Hazlitt**

In the market economy a business must serve others in a beneficial way in order to succeed. That is the beauty of capitalism. In order to profit, you must make your customers' lives better. It's a form of the Golden Rule. This is what the liberal wing of the Democratic Party refuses to understand. The necessity to serve others in order to profit means that free market capitalism holds the moral high ground. Under socialism, no similar requirement exists. Instead of consumers having the free choice of goods and services, they are provided for by government dictate. Whenever that has been tried it has deprived consumers and made them poorer. Nothing can compare with the bounty and product options of capitalism. In the entire history of socialism it has not been able to create a single commercial innovation. Meanwhile, capitalism has showered us with so many material blessings we can't keep track of them. Free markets have eliminated starvation, disease and great swaths of poverty. Furthermore, capitalism creates wealth, opportunities, work and success. As the great Austrian economist Ludwig von Mises (1881-1973) wrote about capitalism, "If you seek its monument look around you." In other words, the blessings of capitalism are all around us every day in every way.

You can only have true freedom under the market economy. This is the ethic of the Yankee peddler to offer you goods and for you to pick and choose if you so decide. In the market economy the consumers are the kings and queens. Their buying decisions determine what companies succeed or fail. Any interference by the government means a reduction of buying choices. That's another way of saying reduced freedoms. A business owner's motives may well be selfish but the consumers are merciless and a business must serve them well or perish. It's as near to a perfect system as humanity will ever achieve.

The entrepreneur Steve Jobs operating within the market system changed our lives. Despite all this evidence liberals and socialists continue to denigrate the free market. They argue for redistribution, high taxes and more government control. They disdain capitalism. They cannot see the benefits of a free market because their core beliefs are false. They are harbingers of retrogression, poverty, despair and national ruin.

We hear them chatter incessantly about income inequality. They push the idea that the market systems bear responsibility for the rich getting richer while the middle class suffers. In reality it is their socialist schemes and intrusions into the market that hurt us. Liberals promote big government despite its detrimental impact on our economy. Look at what these liberals have saddled us with. Start with unions. The left passed laws that allowed unions to get a stranglehold on major industries. At one time the automakers dominated world markets. By 1980 Japanese cars had replaced U.S. cars the world over. Union work rules, lush benefits, and impossibly high wages for unskilled workers made it easy for the competition to overtake us.

YOU CAN ONLY HAVE TRUE FREEDOM UNDER THE MARKET ECONOMY. THIS IS THE ETHIC OF THE YANKEE PEDDLER TO OFFER YOU GOODS AND FOR YOU TO PICK AND CHOOSE IF YOU SO DECIDE.

We've condensed the following comments by author Mark Hendrickson on wealth creation. "The profits that entrepreneurs earn are vilified, falsely slandered as "unearned wealth" (a vestige of ignorant Marxian dogma) and signs of the moral depravity of greed (as if wanting to keep your own property is somehow greedier than other people clamoring for government to give them more of other people's wealth).

"What do the huge profits of successful entrepreneurs really represent? Unlike fortunes that the political elite accumulate in economically rigged systems like feudalism, mercantilism and socialism, in a free-market economy characterized by voluntary, and therefore positive-sum, transactions, the profits of entrepreneurs signify that at least that much wealth has been created for their customers.

"In other words, the larger profits are, the more wealth the entrepreneur has created for others, and indeed, the largest profits accrue to those firms that have supplied valuable goods and services to the masses. How perverse that this precious talent for raising the standards of living of others induces those envious, resentful souls on the left to paint a bull's-eye on the back of those wealth creators and make them targets for government to confiscate more of the profits they justly earned in service to others.

"Here is a historical fact that too few Americans recognize: The profit-seeking entrepreneur – not any government, church, charity or other worthy entity – deserves the credit for lifting us out of poverty and creating our material abundance. We should be grateful for entrepreneurs. They are our economic benefactors, the wealth creators who have enriched our lives."

CHAPTER 2

THE ROAD TO PERDITION

"Trying to get government to be as efficient as business is as hopeless as trying to teach cats to bark and dogs to meow."
Walter Williams

The far left union boss Andy Stern, now a senior fellow at Columbia University, wrote in *The Wall Street Journal* of the need to abandon belief in a free market "The free market fundamentalist economic model is being thrown onto the scrap heap of history." Marx and Lenin couldn't have put it better.

Naive socialist that he is Mr. Stern advises, "America needs to embrace a plan for growth and innovation, with a streamlined government as a partner with the private sectors." We already have government as a partner. They take 50% of everything we earn. "Streamlined government" is the ultimate oxymoron.
There never has been such an animal. How do you streamline a government that is filled with unmotivated bureaucrats?

A business measures results through profit or loss. Government has no such objective standard. They have no bottom line so there is no incentive for cost cutting or sound financial management. Government officials measure results by how much money they spend. Attempts to cut waste and make the bureaucracy more efficient are futile. Government cannot be streamlined. Despite the promise of every new president in the last 100 years to make government work more efficiently it has become an out-of-control monstrosity spending us into oblivion and intervening more clumsily than ever.

Government employees are often promoted solely because of their educational degrees. Merit takes a back seat to political motives, credentials and not rocking the boat. Bureaucratic management has more rules and regulations then does private business because the law imposes restrictions on arbitrary government authority. There is no room for discretion or independent thinking. Common sense takes a back seat to the letter of the law. These rigid and inflexible policies destroy innovation and creativity. Further complications arise when people are given jobs and promotions based on race and gender rather than ability or talent. Such a system can overlook the deserving and reward the incompetent.

Private enterprise must constantly struggle to become more efficient and cost-effective. That's why business pays close attention to the work ethic and merit of the employees. Government pays little or no attention to these crucial elements of business success. By some estimates, private enterprise is five to ten times more efficient than government.

When the government redistributes as much money as it does, the nation becomes a hotbed of politics. Special interest groups elbow up to the government trough. Lobbyists maneuver to cash in on the bounty in Washington. Politicians and bureaucrats who control the purse strings become media stars. Payola and corruption rise. Politics flourish. The body politic and its army of ward heelers won't give up these juicy spoils. The beneficiaries of the social welfare system and the other recipients of government spending will fight to the bitter end to maintain these privileges.

The government bureaucracy never will and never can be reformed or made efficient.

The economic failures that liberals rail against are not failures of free market capitalism. They are failures brought about by government intrusion into the market. Just one example will serve. For centuries the market determined what money was (gold and silver). Now government controls the money and that currency has lost 98% of its purchasing power in my lifetime. This accounts for the destruction of our national savings and a diminishing middle class. Yet progressives can only think of printing more.

The liberal formula for American success is rather the blueprint for national ruin. That so many Americans have bought into this deeply flawed case against free market capitalism is a national tragedy. Over one hundred years ago America's economy experienced a long period of phenomenal growth. It was a time of low taxes, limited government, and minimal regulation. Per capita income, life expectancy and living standards soared. The free market unleashed its blessings. Now we are going in the opposite direction.

CHAPTER 3

DESTROYING WEALTH

"When government taxes and regulates, what is seen are the visible effects of government contracts, grants, and subsidies. What is not seen are all of the property, business, and jobs that would have been created if citizens were left with the right to choose." **John A. Pugsley**

High taxes destroy wealth. Low taxes create wealth. When entrepreneurs keep more of what they earn it enables them to innovate and market thus expanding their enterprises and creating jobs, profits and wealth. We're never going to restore our economic vigor and bail out the middle class until we quit passing out free stuff and cut taxes to the bone.

Liberals like Paul Krugman of *The New York Times* heavily promote high taxes that are little more than a form of wealth confiscation. The pro-capitalist thinker Andrew Galambos (1924-1997) criticized it this way, "People who make more are taxed more. That's being punished for being more productive. And then you're being rewarded for being a parasite. If you don't do anything, if you're just a bum, why, you can go on relief. You get something for nothing. That's a violation of rationality and morality in the short run too. The less you do, the more you get. The more you do, the more you're punished. That's a fine standard for a culture! The most productive people are punished the most for being productive; the ones who produce the least are rewarded for being parasites. Now, if I tried to design an irrational structure of a society, this is exactly what I'd pick."

The great economist Ludwig von Mises could have been writing about liberal politicians when he wrote, "Nothing is more calculated to make a demagogue popular than a constantly reiterated demand for heavy taxes on the rich. Capital levies and high income taxes on the larger incomes are extraordinary popular with the masses, who do not have to pay them."

Leonard Read (1898-1983) founded the Foundation for Economic Education and wrote

29 books. In her biography of Read, Mary Sennholz wrote that after the Second World War Read "rallied the demoralized forces of individual freedom." In 1946 Mr. Read wrote, "More and more people are coming to believe that the free market should be shelved and that, in its stead, government should use its police force to take the income of some and give it to the government's idea of the needy." He continued, "There is no moral difference between the act of a pickpocket and the progressive income tax or any other social program."

HIGH TAXES DESTROY WEALTH. LOW TAXES CREATE WEALTH. WHEN ENTREPRENEURS KEEP MORE OF WHAT THEY EARN IT ENABLES THEM TO INNOVATE AND MARKET THUS EXPANDING THEIR ENTERPRISES AND CREATING JOBS, PROFITS AND WEALTH.

Does any able adult person 'in need' really benefit by living on the confiscated income of others? Does this ever improve his character or his mental and physical faculties? His growth? Does anyone ever benefit by the removal of self-responsibility?"

Leonard Read argued that taking the earnings of people through taxation and giving it to people who didn't earn it was an evil act that committed us to its retribution. He claimed, "There is no greater dishonesty than man effecting his own private gains at the expense of others." Mr. Read thought that government welfare "must lead to an evil end to those who live on it."

Of the tax collectors, government regulators and bureaucrats he wrote, "I cannot indulge in my own upgrading at the same time I am inhibiting someone else's creative action. Therefore, to the extent that one's life is spent in using force to coerce others, to that extent is one's life destroyed and its higher purpose frustrated ... Nothing creative is induced by compulsion."

Leonard Read suggested that private charity was instrumental in making a society great. Under capitalism the charitable acts of private individuals would grow and flourish thus eliminating many of societies' ills. But with income redistribution these bonds of brotherhood are crushed by government compulsion. Bureaucrats decide who gets what at the expense of private giving and charity. This kind of socialism, he suggested, would cause our nation to "fly apart."

Because socialism relies on compulsion, Leonard Read stood firmly against it. He wrote, "Socialism takes and redistributes wealth, but it is utterly incapable of creating wealth." He warned, "Man cannot feign the role of God without finally playing the devil's part." His most profound criticism of government regarded its constant inflating. "Inflation makes the extension of socialism possible by providing the financial chaos in which it flourishes. The fact is that socialism and inflation are simultaneously cause and effect; they feed on each other!"

Firing a warning shot across the bow of Washington and Wall Street he quoted a wise man. "Ultimately with God's aid, truth always emerges and finally prevails, supreme in its power over the destiny of mankind, and terrible is the retribution for those who deny, defy, or betray it." That's how Leonard Read saw it. Big government and socialism would cause our economy to disintegrate. Unfortunately, this nearsighted nation ignores any such warnings. It behooves each of us to give Leonard Read's disturbing arguments the most careful thought.

CHAPTER 4

DESTROYING WESTERN CIVILIZATION

"Somehow, the fact that more poor people are on welfare, receiving more generous payments, does not seem to have made this country a nice place to live – not even for the poor on welfare, whose condition seems not noticeably better than when they were poor and off welfare. Something appears to have gone wrong; a liberal and compassionate social policy has bred all sorts of unanticipated and perverse consequences."
Irving Kristol

As long as the government gives poor people money, they have little or no incentive to escape the dole and improve their economic fate. Their job skills never develop and the qualities needed for employment erode. Over time welfare recipients become unemployable and essentially helpless. It's the dole or die. Most of the talking heads on TV proclaim a need for jobs and better opportunities for the poor. However, as long as the government checks and other subsidies keep coming, very few will have the talent or the will to escape.

The author Llewellyn Rockwell wrote, "America's 20th-century experiment with the welfare state desolated our cities, created a permanent underclass of promiscuity, illegitimacy, welfare and crime, and gave us children and adults full of race hatred instead of the social discipline and work ethic necessary to civilization."

In a 1995 article I wrote, "In the past 50 years trillions of dollars have been transferred to the poor. Surely a sum this vast should have made inroads against poverty. However, these trillions in entitlements have been accompanied by an astronomical increase in criminal behavior, a runaway plague of alcohol and drug addiction and a stupendous breakdown in the family unit. Trillions directed at poverty have led to an astonishing increase in the numbers of poor and an explosion of street people and homeless." These days welfare dollars are also contributing mightily to the drug crisis by indirectly transferring our tax dollars to drug cartels.

In discussing high crime rates and other pathologies of the poor, the linkage to free money is never talked about. The dole causes a virulent boredom responsible for social mayhem, addiction and gross neglect of family responsibilities. Bad character grows worse from generation to generation. The subsidized life without work or purpose is a curse for the victim and for society. The problem will only get worse if new immigrants fall into the welfare trap.

Eliminating welfare becomes impossible because so many have come to rely on it. It can't be peeled back and it grows like the runaway malignancy that it is. Since the costs are running away, it's reasonable to ask, is there a breaking point? Will there be a time when the welfare checks bounce or don't buy anything? How will our massive subsidized population react if their money gets taken away? It could be ugly and dangerous. Free money is not only a trap for the individual; it's a trap for our civilization.

The late management guru Peter Drucker said, "The evidence is thus crystal-clear. Modern welfare destroys. Despite ever larger and constantly growing expenditures, the 'welfare mess' in the United States is getting steadily worse. In fact, a strong case can be made – and has been made – that the poor in America ... have become poorer, the more helpless, the more disadvantaged, the more welfare money is being spent on them. American welfare spending encourages dependence. It paralyzes rather than energizes."

Twenty trillion spent on social welfare has not mitigated the poverty problem. However, it has sponsored an enormous increase in drug use, alcohol dependence and bizarre anti-social behavior. These pathologies are ruinous. Think of the medical costs of eighty-one gunshot wounds in one Chicago weekend. Add up the salaries of the public defenders, judges and court system. Think of the costs of policing, imprisonment and paroling. First the government spends on subsidies, then it spends even more on the damage done by the subsidies.

The ultimate heresy in progressive America is to suggest that the government shouldn't subsidize anybody. However it's been mentioned before. James Madison, a founding father said, "I cannot undertake to lay my finger on that article of the Constitution which granted a right to

Congress of expending, on objects of benevolence, the money of their constituents." In his 1968 free market seminar the physicist Andrew Galambos said, "I want to point out that welfare and destitution are not alternates; they're the same thing. It is the welfare program, this bleeding heart so-called 'humanitarianism,' that creates destitution."

In 1966 the author Robert Ardrey wrote a controversial inquiry into the nature of man entitled, "The Territorial Imperative." Ardrey wrote that there are three principal needs of all higher animals, including man: the need for identity, the need for stimulation and the need for security. Beyond these three, he could find no others. Ardrey wrote, "Identity, stimulation, security; if you think of them in terms of their opposites their images will be sharpened. Identity is the opposite of anonymity. Stimulation is the opposite of boredom. Security is the opposite of anxiety. We shun anonymity, dread boredom, and seek to dispel anxiety. We grasp at identification, yearn for stimulation, conserve or gain security."

"There are few exceptions," he wrote, "to the rule that the need for identity is the most powerful and most pervasive among all species. The need for stimulation is not far behind. And security, normally, will be sacrificed for either of the other two." Then ominously for the

ELIMINATING WELFARE BECOMES IMPOSSIBLE BECAUSE SO MANY HAVE COME TO RELY ON IT. IT CAN'T BE PEELED BACK AND IT GROWS LIKE THE RUNAWAY MALIGNANCY THAT IT IS.

American welfare state he wrote, "The structure of security is the birthplace of boredom ... Our means of satisfying innate needs are precious few, and sacrifice of any must mean replacement by another."

Writing in a biology book in the mid-60's, almost as though he could foretell the failed future of the "The Great Society," Robert Ardrey stated, "We may agree, for example that our societies must provide greater security for the individual; yet if all we succeed in producing is a social structure providing increased anonymity and ever increasing boredom, then we should not wonder if ingenious man turns to such amusements as drugs, housebreaking, vandalism, mayhem, riots, or – at the most harmless –

strange haircuts, costumes, standards of cleanliness, and sexual experiments." Nowhere else has anyone written a more apt description of the welfare predicament.

Government does not cure poverty, government creates poverty. Our citizens' growing participation in social welfare programs fosters government deficits and impossible levels of spending. Providing something for nothing poisons our society and corrupts our culture. Unearned money destroys the work ethic and ruins the character and habits of the recipients. Nevertheless, politicians on the left demand more. Meanwhile the numbers of poor people grow and their pathologies worsen. This is how the end of Western civilization begins.

TWENTY TRILLION SPENT ON SOCIAL WELFARE HAS NOT MITIGATED THE POVERTY PROBLEM. HOWEVER, IT HAS SPONSORED AN ENORMOUS INCREASE IN DRUG USE, ALCOHOL DEPENDENCE AND BIZARRE ANTI-SOCIAL BEHAVIOR.

CHAPTER 5

NATIONAL SUICIDE

"It is the highest impertinence and presumption, therefore, in kings and ministers, to pretend to watch over the economy of private people, and to restrain their expense ... (Kings and ministers) are themselves always, and without any exception, the greatest spendthrifts in the society. Let them look well after their own expense, and they may safely trust private people with theirs. If their own extravagance does not ruin the state, that of their subjects never will." **Adam Smith**

In 1979, after six years, my company Investment Rarities made its first profit. I was shocked when we had to give 40% of it to the IRS and the state. That was our cushion that could help us survive future bad years. To this day, I believe many companies that failed would still be in business if taxes were lower. High taxes kill business. They penalize progress. That's just one of the many things liberal government does that harms our economy.

Every time the government lays down a new law or regulation, it has the potential for serious damage. Business invests enormous energy in complying with new rules. Management's attention to regulations and red tape detracts from a company's efficiency. A single regulation can exterminate an entire industry. Regulators are a police force intent on tripping up errant businesses, levying fines or worse. Nowadays people sue corporations at the drop of a hat. U.S. businesses spend too much time and money defending against litigation. Suits emanating from the government can paralyze a company for years. America desperately needs tort reform.

Welfare, unemployment benefits and other subsidies weaken the work force. Some workers will slough off, report late, miss work or abuse chemicals if they know a government check will replace their paycheck. The government provides incentives to goof off. People would also save more if it weren't for these programs. Low savings means we spend more and invest less. Our social safety net helps kill savings.

Our industries lose ground to foreign competitors who

A SINGLE REGULATION CAN EXTERMINATE AN ENTIRE INDUSTRY. REGULATORS ARE A POLICE FORCE INTENT ON TRIPPING UP ERRANT BUSINESSES, LEVYING FINES OR WORSE.

undersell us. The main expense of any business is labor. Foreign competition enjoys lower labor costs. Our unions may crow about raising wages, but they also price companies out of the market and cause job loss. Government subsidies to certain businesses favor their success against competitors. Legal barriers to starting a business such as permits, bonds, licenses or regulations help big companies fend off competitors. Government intervention stifles competition. Government-sponsored inflation, extreme currency fluctuations, the boom and bust cycle, and dollar devaluations all make doing business more difficult. Government attempts to improve the economy waste capital. They distort pricing and interest rates.

The government has fostered a national ethic of getting something for nothing. This burdens business with phony lawsuits, employee theft, trumped up medical claims, insurance fraud and poor character. Business pays for all or part of health care costs, unemployment benefits, workers' compensation insurance, product liability insurance, Social Security and Medicare. When you add non-productive legal costs, licensing fees, property taxes, sales tax, income tax, excise taxes and the world's highest corporate tax, you have a thoroughbred carrying a 300-pound jockey. In other parts of the world they don't have to carry this much weight.

The sentiments of most government employees and the bureaucrats who enforce the rules are fiercely anti-business. They have little or no knowledge of how the market system works. They see business as greed-driven and profits as an evil that government should control.

An anti-business attitude proliferates in the media. Both T.V. and cinema portray business leaders as criminals. The press, magazine, and book publishers are infested with writers expressing a dislike of capitalism. Church leaders reflect these same sentiments. Professors and teachers sneer at the system that has given them the highest living standard in history. The deck is stacked against free enterprise. So that is how our great country is committing hara-kiri. These trends are not going to end until they ruin us. Nothing will stop the government from taxing and spending until the dollar is destroyed. Nothing will keep them from sending out endless checks to the subsidized but national bankruptcy. It's all downhill from here and you should be afraid to know what's at the bottom.

You can't begin to imagine how much money is frittered away on useless government initiatives. In Minneapolis, last month an organization called Northside Achievement Zone won a $28 million dollar federal grant to improve an impoverished neighborhood. A group of liberals were pictured in the newspaper applauding and our two left-wing Senators were on hand. Certainly the supporters mean well but the fact that throwing money at the problem doesn't work never seems to register.

The CEO was in tears as she pointed out the many needs of the neighborhood. This is an area of high crime, drugs, alcoholism, broken families, prostitution and delinquency. Most of these people are subsidized and on welfare. Trillions have been spent trying to cure neighborhoods like this and if anything, they have grown worse. It's highly likely that federal subsidies are more the cause of these behavioral problems than the cure. If you don't have to work, boredom begets pathologies.

As for the $28 million I put it in perspective this way. Since 1973 when I started my company we have had up to 300 employees (in 1980). All of us have worked hard to improve our circumstances. We have all paid taxes in a timely fashion. In all those 38 years of hard work all of us have probably paid the government close to $28 million. It takes a lot of effort to get that amount of taxes. Nevertheless, the government dispenses it with little realization of the work and struggle involved.

It wouldn't be so bad if they were just spending our tax money. They can't get along on that. They have to borrow the $28 million and if they've borrowed too much they will have to print the $28 million. Multiply that a thousand times over and you will see why we are dead in the water.

CHAPTER 6

THE ECONOMICS OF ARMAGEDDON

"Inflationism is a dreadful cancer that is gnawing at the backbone of the civilized order."
Hans F. Sennholz

Whenever I'm stuck over something to write in my newsletter, I dig out my dog-eared volume of *Human Action* by the Austrian School economist Ludwig von Mises (1881-1973). This great economist warned time and again about the sorry consequences of our left-wing monetary policies. Although he passed from the scene in 1973, he was prescient enough to write, "Radical inflationism is an essential feature of the economic ideology of our age." Mises was death on inflating. He wrote that it was a policy that could not last. Ultimately, it must lead to hyperinflation or an economic bust.

In 1967 he wrote, "Inflationism is a government policy of increasing the quantity of money in order to enable the government to spend more than the funds provided by taxation and borrowing. Such 'deficit spending' is nowadays, as everybody knows the characteristic signature of the U.S. government's policies." He added, "There is no reason to be proud of deficit spending or to call it progress."

Mises' main complaint against this inflating was the damage it did to the people who saved. In 1960 he wrote, "One of the main achievements of the capitalistic system is the opportunity it offers to the masses of citizens to save and thereby improve their material well-being ... the value of all kinds of deposits, bonds and insurance policies is inseparably linked to the purchasing power of the dollar. A policy of creeping inflation ... is a policy against the vital material interests of the common man. It hurts seriously those judicious and conscientious earners of wages and salaries who are intent upon improving their own and their families' lot by thrift ... It is ... diabolic ... for more and more government spending to be financed by credit expansion.

The bill for such government extravagance is always footed by the most industrious and provident people. It is their claims [savings] that are shrinking with the dollar's purchasing power."

During Mises' lifetime he saw the arguments of John Maynard Keynes become influential. In 1951 Mises wrote, "The triumphs of Lord Keynes' last book, *The General Theory*, was instantaneous ... it has become the gospel of the self-styled progressives all over the world. Today many universities simply teach Keynesianism. It is really paradoxical. Nobody can any longer fail to realize what is needed most is more saving and capital accumulation and that the inflationary and expansionist polices are on the verge of complete breakdown. But the students are still taught the dangers of saving and the blessing of inflating."

He wrote, "Continued inflation inevitably leads to catastrophe." He indicted Washington, "It is government interference that has destroyed money in the past and it is government interference that is destroying money again." Mises also scorned politicians, Treasury and Federal Reserve officials who claimed to be intent on thwarting inflation.

"Those who pretend to fight inflation are in fact only fighting the inevitable consequences of inflation, rising prices ... They try to keep prices low while firmly committed to a policy of increasing the quantity of money that must necessarily make them soar."

"INFLATIONISM IS NOT A VARIETY OF ECONOMIC POLICIES. IT IS AN INSTRUMENT OF DESTRUCTION ..."

He culminated his arguments against inflating with dire warnings on where the monetary policies of today will lead. Bear in mind that Mises through his many books and trenchant arguments is recognized as a towering genius in his field. "It must be remembered that inflation is not a policy that can last. If inflation and credit expansion are not stopped in time, they result in a more and more accelerated drop in the monetary unit's purchasing power, and in skyrocketing commodity prices until the inflated money becomes entirely worthless and the whole government-manipulated currency system collapses. In our age, this has happened to the monetary regime of various countries."

He further warned, "Inflationism is not a variety of economic policies. It is an instrument of destruction; if not stopped very soon, it destroys the market entirely." Finally, here are Mises' comments that apply to the Krugmanites, progressive politicians and the Washington monetary gang: "Inflationism cannot last; if not radically stopped in time, it must lead inexorably to a complete breakdown. It is an expedient of people who do not care a whit for the future of their nation and its civilization. It is the policy of Madame de Pompadour, the mistress of the French King Louis XV – Après nous le déluge (after us the deluge)."

He experienced firsthand the Weimar Republic inflation and he explained what happens in a runaway inflation. "The course of progressing inflation is this: at the beginning the inflow of additional money makes the price of some commodities and services rise; other prices rise later. The price rise affects the various commodities and services at different dates and to a different extent.

"This first stage of the inflationary process may last for years. While it lasts, the prices of many goods and services are not yet adjusted to the altered money relation. There are still people in the country who will not yet become aware of the fact that they are confronted with a price revolution which will finally result in a considerable rise of all prices, although the extent of this rise will not be the same in the various commodities and services.

"Finally, the masses wake up. They become suddenly aware of the fact that inflation is a deliberate policy and will go on endlessly. A breakdown occurs. The crack-up boom appears. Everybody is anxious to swap his money against 'real' goods, no matter how much money he has to pay for them. Within a very short time, within a few weeks or even days, the things which were used as money are no longer used as media of exchange. They become scrap paper. Nobody wants to give away anything against them.

"It was this that happened with the continental currency in America in 1781, with the French mandats territoriaux in 1796, and with the German mark in 1923. It will happen again whenever the same conditions appear. If a thing has to be used as a medium of exchange, public opinion must not believe that the quantity of this thing will increase beyond all bounds."

CHAPTER 7

TRUTH TELLER

"Big government comes at a big cost. This cost most obviously shows in reduced economic growth, fewer jobs, reduced take-home pay, and less overall prosperity. In an era of globalization, when Americans must compete on an international basis, taxation and regulation act as an anchor on American productivity and competitiveness."
Michael D. Tanner

In March of 1945, Ludwig von Mises gave a speech to a group of intellectuals in Philadelphia. The speech could have been given today. He described the liberal agenda. "The interventionists believe that government has the power to improve the masses' standard of living partly at the expense of the capitalists and entrepreneurs, partly at no expense at all. They recommend the restriction of profits and the equalization of incomes and fortunes by confiscatory taxation, the lowering of the rate of interest by an easy money policy and credit expansion, and the raising of the workers' standard of living by the enforcement of minimum wage rates. They advocate lavish government spending."

Countering this progressive viewpoint, Mises wrote, "Those who pretend that they want to preserve freedom, while they are eager to fix prices, wage rates, and interest rates at a level different from that of the market, delude themselves. There is no other alternative to totalitarian slavery than liberty. There is no other planning for freedom and general welfare than to let the market system work. There is no other means to attain full employment, rising real wage rates and a high standard of living for the common man than private initiative and free enterprise."

In 1949 Mises wrote of his experience in the Weimar era hyperinflation. "The recurrence of periods of economic depression is the outcome of the repeated attempts to improve the operation of capitalism by 'cheap money' and credit expansion. If one wants to avert depressions, one must abstain from any tampering with the rate of interest. Thus was elaborated my theory which supporters and critics soon began to call the 'Austrian theory of the trade cycle.'

"As expected, my theses were furiously vilified by the apologists of the official doctrine. Especially abusive was the response on the part of the German professors. In exemplifying one point, a hypothetical assumption was made [by Mises] that the purchasing power of the German mark might drop to one-millionth of its previous equivalent. 'What a muddle-headed man who dares to introduce – if only hypothetically – such a fantastic assumption!' shouted one of the reviewers. But a few years later the purchasing power of the mark was down not to one-millionth, but to one-billionth of its prewar amount!

"It is a sad fact that people are reluctant to learn from either theory or experience. Neither the disasters brought about by deficit spending and low interest rate policies, nor the confirmation of the theories by such eminent thinkers as Friedrich von Hayek, Henry Hazlitt and the late Benjamin M. Anderson have up to now been able to put an end to the popularity of the fiat money frenzy. The monetary policies of all nations are headed for a new catastrophe.

"Money is the phenomenon of the market, a medium of exchange. But governments think of money as a product of government activity. Money is not a creation of the government. This should be repeated again and again. It is government interference that has destroyed money in the past and it is government interference that is destroying money again … A thing cannot serve as money if the government has the right to increase its quantity at its pleasure."

Mises not only advocated free markets, he established the moral foundation that underpins capitalism: "The market economy directs the individual's activities into those channels in which he best serves the wants of his fellow man." He also mistrusted the state. "If government were in a position to expand its power ad libitum, it could abolish the market economy and substitute for it all-round totalitarian socialism. In order to prevent this, it is necessary to curb the power of government. This is the task of all constitutions, bills of rights, and laws. This is the meaning of all struggles which men have fought for liberty."

Most worrisome is Mises' warning about what could happen if Marxism and socialism were to prevail over free market capitalism. "It rests with men whether they will make the proper use of the rich treasure with which this [economic] knowledge provides them or whether they will leave it unused. But if they fail to take the best advantage of it and disregard its teachings and warnings, they will not annul economics; they will stamp out society and the human race."

Mises was the greatest champion of capitalism the world has ever known. Below, we've condensed some of his writings on the subject:

The characteristic feature of modern capitalism is mass production of goods for consumption by the masses. The result is a tendency towards a continuous improvement in the average standard of living. In a capitalistic society it is the common man or woman whose buying ultimately determines what should be produced in what quantity and quality.

Those shops and plants, which cater exclusively to the wealthier citizens' demand for refined luxuries, play merely a subordinate role in the market economy. They never attain the size of big business. Big business always serves – directly or indirectly – the masses.

"MONEY IS THE PHENOMENON OF THE MARKET, A MEDIUM OF EXCHANGE. BUT GOVERNMENTS THINK OF MONEY AS A PRODUCT OF GOVERNMENT ACTIVITY. MONEY IS NOT A CREATION OF THE GOVERNMENT.

The profit system makes those men prosper who have succeeded in filling the wants of the people in the best possible and cheapest way. The entrepreneurs and capitalists owe their wealth to the people who patronize their businesses. They lose it as soon as other men or women supplant them in serving the consumers better or cheaper. Wealth can be acquired only by serving the consumers. The consumers determine who should own and run the plants, shops and farms.

Under capitalism everybody's station of life depends on his or her own doing. Capitalism is essentially a system of mass production for the satisfaction of the needs of the masses. It pours a horn of plenty upon the common man. Under capitalism the common man enjoys amenities, which in ages gone by were unknown and therefore inaccessible even to the richest people. It has raised the average standard of living to a height never dreamed of in earlier ages. It has made accessible to millions of people enjoyments, which a few generations ago were only within the reach of a small elite.

The entrepreneurs who provide the best and cheapest way all the things required for the satisfaction of these wants succeed in getting rich. What counts in the market economy is not academic judgments of value, but the valuations actually manifested by people in buying or not buying. To the grumbler who complains about the unfairness of the market system only one piece of advice can be given: if you want to acquire wealth, then try to satisfy the public by offering them something that is cheaper or which they like better.

CAPITALISM IS ESSENTIALLY A SYSTEM OF MASS PRODUCTION FOR THE SATISFACTION OF THE NEEDS OF THE MASSES. IT POURS A HORN OF PLENTY UPON THE COMMON MAN.

CHAPTER 8

AIR WAR

"Liberals see the Constitution itself as 'living' and 'evolving' – that is, gradually turning into something that would have been unrecognizable to its authors." **Joseph Sobran**

I have this oil painting depicting something unbelievable that happened in World War II. A B-17 was returning from a bombing raid over Germany in 1943. It had been heavily damaged by flak and by fighters. The tail gunner was dead and most of the tail and stabilizer shot away. None of the guns were working. The waist gunner had lost a leg. One engine was out and another acting up. The nose was torn apart and the plane had plummeted thousands of feet to a low level with little chance of making it the 240 miles back to England.

A German fighter pilot with 27 kills to his credit had shot down one B-17 that day and had landed for fuel and ammunition. Suddenly, the crippled B-17 flew directly over his airstrip. He quickly taxied onto the runway and took off after the crippled bomber. As he approached from behind he could see the dead tail gunner and through the holes in the side of the plane he saw the wounded crew huddled together. This would be an easy kill.

He pulled up above the pilot and copilot and looked down at them. They looked up at him in fear. They knew they had no chance. After flying beside them for a few minutes the German pilot suddenly saluted them, peeled off and let them go. A few hours later the badly damaged bomber made it back to England.

Fast forward 40 years to a reunion in Florida. The German pilot and the American pilot met with tears in their eyes. The American crew knew that the German pilot had risked his life by letting them go that day. Twenty-five children and grandchildren of the surviving crew gathered around the German pilot and thanked him for their lives.

27

The painting is on the cover of a book that was published recently telling this story. It is titled *A Higher Call*, by Adam Makos. The book and the painting were also featured in the *New York Post*. I started to read it on a recent flight. It's a beautiful, interesting story.

In describing the German pilot's early life I found some interesting facts. Hitler had only received 44% of the vote in 1932. A majority voted against him. Nevertheless, the Nazis escalated a reign of terror, killing all who criticized them. The leaders of the Catholic Church in Germany placed themselves in grave danger by criticizing the Nazis. The pilot who let the B-17 go was grilled by the S.S. during the war for his family's Catholicism. It got so bad that a woman was killed for telling the following joke: "Hitler and Goering were standing on a tall building. Hitler asked Goering what he could do to help the German people. Jump, replied Goering." They hanged her.

There were no checks and balances in Germany. They had no constitution with separation of powers. Their legislative, executive and judicial branches did not balance one another. Had Germany a constitution similar to ours, Hitler couldn't have happened. Russia's communists had a sweet sounding constitution based on social justice, but that did not keep the murderous Stalin at bay. Two important branches of their government were weak.

Our Constitution is the most important document on earth. It has proven itself time and again. That is why when liberals want to change it into a so-called "living document," we must resist. Typical of liberal mischief is a recent bill in the Senate supported by every Democrat that would alter the first amendment. Our forefathers knew what they were doing. If the left manages to change our Constitution it opens the door to barbarism. Spread the word, the liberal agenda is the blueprint for national ruin.

CHAPTER 9

JOB CREATION

"No matter whether it is their intention or not, almost anything that the rich can legally do tends to help the poor. The spending of the rich gives employment to the poor. But the saving of the rich, and their investment of these savings in the means of production, gives just as much employment, and in addition makes that employment constantly more productive and more highly paid, while it also constantly increases and cheapens the production of necessities and amenities for the masses." **Henry Hazlitt**

I started my company Investment Rarities in 1973. We had a brief run in 1974 when gold and silver jumped up but by 1975 it was over. The first energy crisis had dawned and we survived by developing and selling the Sierra Wood Burning Stove. We began to publish the *Wood Burning Quarterly*, which sold in fireplace stores.
In time, we changed the name to *Home Energy Digest* and wrote extensively about solar energy, wind power, biomass and other forms of alternative energy. The government was pouring money into all of them in the form of grants, subsidies and tax breaks. Nothing much came of it. The government wasted a lot of money.

One day I got a call from an engineer who read our magazine. He made an appointment to see me. During his visit he explained that he and 70 others were being paid by the government to come up with solutions to the energy crisis. It had been two years and thus far they hadn't hit upon anything. My advice was to develop an energy-saving product that people would buy. Apparently that had never dawned on them because he thought it was a great idea. My distaste for government solutions went up a notch after this meeting. I knew they would never come up with anything and the government was wasting money on endless projects like this across the nation. Today they are force-feeding billions of dollars to create green jobs. I've seen this act before. It doesn't work.

29

The government thinks if they take enough money from the people who earn it and subsidize a bunch of people this will create millions of jobs. How dumb are they? Let me tell you what it takes to create jobs. Someone has to turn their back on their financial security, step away from a regular paycheck and risk everything on a business venture. They have to undergo days and nights of racking anxiety, work and struggle for months without gain and skirt the edge of failure while finding the will to persist.

THE GOVERNMENT THINKS IF THEY TAKE ENOUGH MONEY FROM THE PEOPLE WHO EARN IT AND SUBSIDIZE A BUNCH OF PEOPLE THIS WILL CREATE MILLIONS OF JOBS. HOW DUMB ARE THEY?

If they can survive this relentless adversity and be creative enough to develop a product or service that people want they can begin to break even and eventually hire someone. That creates one job. No matter how many employees a company eventually has, that's how it starts. Is there anyone in Washington who understands what it takes to create one job?

For every new business that succeeds there are fifty that don't last five years. Those who survive and begin to make a profit are in for a rude awakening. The precious capital they've managed to earn gets quickly taxed away by the government. This is money that would otherwise be used to create growth and employment. A business strives to gain a financial cushion that will help them survive a slump or downturn. However, state and federal taxes take half of their profits thereby causing them to fail, stunting employment and killing jobs.

There's a formula for job creation. Let businesses keep more of what they earn. Most especially let business startups go without taxes. For an immediate turnaround cut all business taxes to the bone. Make it highly profitable to take risks that create jobs. Unleash the entrepreneurs and get the government out of the way.

CHAPTER 10

NAUSEATING

"Once we realize that government doesn't work, we will stop dreaming that this or that social program can be solved by passing a law – or by creating a new government program – or by electing someone who will make Washington more efficient or cost conscious." **Harry Browne**

Apparently politics and government have become the most important thing in America. The news organizations dwell on the utterances of the chief executive as if he were Moses. Politicians of all persuasions are featured in the news. The government's many social initiatives are covered microscopically in the media. Much of the nation appears to worship the state. It's as if our government, the bureaucrats and the politicians have become our saviors. Frankly, it's sickening. A growing government threatens to diminish our freedoms and exterminate our prosperity. We are so far down the road to socialism, there appears to be no turning back. Apparently, the majority have drank the Kool-Aid. So prepare to be inundated with political news and unending praise for the government and its programs.

Ludwig von Mises understood the evils of big government. He wrote, "Government means always coercion and compulsion and is by necessity the opposite of liberty." On government redistribution he wrote, "The truth is the government cannot give if it does not take from somebody." He exposed the government's shortcomings. "Daily experience proves clearly to everybody but the most bigoted fanatics of socialism that government management is inefficient and wasteful."

Mises explained the growth of government this way: "The essence of statism is to take from one group in order to give to another. The more it can take, the more it can give. It is to the interest of those whom the government wishes to favor that the state becomes as large as possible." Mises also explained why we are subjected

31

to a constant steam of political propaganda. "It is characteristic of current political thinking to welcome every suggestion which aims at enlarging the influence of government."

Where is this public love affair with big government taking us? We can tune out the media blitz, but we can't undo the damage from the inroads of liberalism and socialism. For me the inevitable outcome is national bankruptcy. Out of that can come either a reduced leviathan and a rebirth of freedom, or some sort of supersized government police state. As Mises reminds us, "Liberty is always freedom from government."

Mises understood that there must always be government. It was the degree the state intervened in economic freedom that was the litmus test. The proper role of good government was to protect the citizens from criminals, defend against foreign enemies and ensure the smooth operation of the market economy. These limitations are ignored today. To which Mises warned, "There is no hope left for a civilization when the masses favor harmful policies."

CHAPTER 11

WHAT LIBERALS CAN'T COMPREHEND

"Achievement is not what liberalism is about. Victimhood and dependency are."
Thomas Sowell

Liberal social programs destroy human initiative. They eliminate the need to struggle. Instead of getting tougher and smarter, the subsidized get weaker. I learned early in my business career the necessity of struggle and persistence. Although I encountered what seemed like insurmountable problems, it turned out that the solution was always available. In my book *The Start-Up Entrepreneur*, I quoted Lee De Forest, the inventor of the vacuum tube: "There were some times when I felt as if I had gone my limit. Some of my setbacks were stunners. It seemed as if I couldn't get the stamina to start again. But every time, when I studied things over a little, I would find a way out. No matter how hopeless things look, there is always a way out if you look for it hard enough."

That's why government programs are so damaging. They pull the rug out from under the people they supposedly help. Liberal social programs make people helpless. As the great motivational author Napoleon Hill put it, "We are forced to recognize that this universal necessity for struggle must have a definite and useful purpose. That purpose is to force the individual to sharpen his wits, arouse his enthusiasm, build up his spirit of faith, gain definiteness of purpose, develop his power of will, inspire his faculty of imagination to give him new uses for old ideas and concepts, and thereby fulfill some unknown mission for which he or she may have been born.

"Strength, both physical and spiritual, is the product of struggle! 'Do the thing,' said Emerson, 'and you shall have the power.' Meet struggle and master it, says nature, and you shall have strength and wisdom sufficient for all your needs. In every form of life, atrophy and death come from idleness! The only thing nature will not tolerate is idleness. There may be some pain in most forms of struggle, but nature compensates the individual for the pain in the form of power and strength and wisdom which come from practical experience."

Napoleon Hill wrote, "When any individual reconciles himself to the state of mind wherein he is willing to accept largesse from the government, instead of supplying his needs through personal initiative, that individual is on the road to decay and spiritual blindness. When a majority of the people of any nation give up their inherited prerogative right to make their own way through struggle, history shows clearly that the entire nation is in a tailspin of decay that inevitably must end in extinction. The individual who not only is willing to live on the public treasury, but demands that he be fed from it, is already dead spiritually."

Liberals are blind to the wisdom in these paragraphs. What's the matter with them? Do they have a death wish for our country? This is the main reason America is in so much trouble. Too many people are taking the easy way out. Progressives have absolutely no insight into the damage they do. Their runaway social sympathy sentences people to a miserable life.

A century ago an author by the name of Glenville Kleiser wrote these words: "The worst thing that can befall you is to have nothing useful to do. From that moment life will be an aimless, aching void, and time a cruel torturer. The man who has not experienced the joy of hard work has lived in vain. A life of ease and sloth is a daily purgatory and a cause of widespread unhappiness. It is incomprehensible that in this day of golden opportunity there should be anyone, in good health, with nothing to work and live for. The joy of work, of daily conquest, of unexpected difficulties overcome, of new enterprises – these make life interesting, worthwhile and wholesome. Find your right vocation, put your best abilities to daily use, work cheerfully, willingly, and courageously, and you will know the joy of true living."

This poem by Ella Wheeler Wilcox sums it up beautifully:

Three Things

Know this, ye restless denizens of earth,
Know this, ye seekers after joy and mirth,
Three things there are, eternal in their worth.

Love that outreaches to the humblest things;
Work that is glad, in what it

*does and brings;
And faith that soars upon
unwearied wings.*

*Divine the powers that on this
trio wait.
Supreme their conquest, over
Time and Fate.
Love, Work, Faith – these three
alone are great.*

Every once in a while I switch the TV channel from Fox to CNBC to see what the liberals are saying. After listening awhile I get a deep sense of hopelessness and foreboding for our country. The most important thing for the left is giving money to people. They are happy to see the growth of food stamps, disability payments, housing subsidies, free health care and all the other welfare benefits. They utterly fail to see the damage it is doing to the recipients. Whole cities that once flourished have deteriorated into rotting eyesores populated with shambling hulks of chemically dependent drones. These people are no longer employable. They have become incompetent and helpless and the liberals can't see that it's their doing.

Furthermore, each new wave of subsidized citizens (and immigrants) promises to ultimately fall into the same behavioral sinkhole – if not them, their offspring who will quickly learn to embrace the subsidized life. We hear only that the bad economy is propelling the growth in government handouts. We never hear that the subsidized life is easier, softer and without challenge. We never hear that it is the opposite of ambition, struggle and growth.

This curse on our nation's character goes hand-in-hand with the debt and inflation that's necessary to pay for it. We risk debasing the dollar paying for government subsidies. Loose money turns a nation into speculators and spenders rather than producers and savers. Throw in the government's many other socialist schemes and you have the mess we are in. It's getting worse. The culture and the people are growing coarser. The productive citizens will soon be in the minority if they are not already. The nation has lost its way and the left so widely chronicled in the media bears responsibility.

Someday the free lunch will have to end. The government will no longer have the means to pay for it. A bankrupt nation with a bankrupt culture; that's what these so-called progressives are saddling us with. Their runaway social sympathy has brought us a permanent crisis and the erosion of our prosperity and greatness. They are the architects of our downfall.

CHAPTER 12

THE ECONOMIST WHO SAW THE FUTURE

"'Need' now means wanting someone else's money. 'Greed' means wanting to keep your own. 'Compassion' is when a politician arranges the transfer."
Joseph Sobran

Hans Sennholz (1922-2007) was a professor of economics and a student of Ludwig von Mises while at NYU. Professor Sennholz was an intrepid critic of government deficits. "If we cannot return to fiscal integrity because the public prefers prodigality over balanced budgets, we cannot escape paying the price, which is ever lower incomes and standards of living for all. The pains of economic stagnation and decline, which are plaguing us today, are likely to intensify and multiply in the coming years. The social and racial conflict, which springs from the redistribution ideology, may deepen as economic output is shrinking and transfer 'entitlements' cause budget deficits to soar. The U.S. dollar, which has become a mere corollary of government finance, is unlikely to survive the soaring deficits."

He explained how government deficits grow. "When the public demand for government services and benefits grows beyond the ability of business and wealthy taxpayers to pay, budgetary deficits become unavoidable. The popularity of redistribution by political force tends to grow in every dollar of 'free' service rendered. The clamor finally becomes so intense that, in order to be heard, every new call is presented as an 'emergency' that must be met immediately before all others. Redistributive government then rushes from one emergency to another, trying to meet the most noise and politically potent demands."

On the subject of debt he wrote, "The man who lives above his present circumstances is in great danger of soon living much beneath them. The same is true with a group of people called 'society.' To live beyond its means is to invite poverty and deprivation. Deficit spending consumes wealth, engages in mass deceit about economic reality, sets a poor example to others, makes people dependent and subservient, causes uncertainty and instability, and breeds social conflict and strife. It may even weaken the political institutions of a free society."

He argued that the capital consumed by government would have been better spent in private hands. "It is difficult to estimate the number of factories and stores that were not built, the tools and dies that were not cast, the jobs not created, the wages not paid, the food, clothing and shelter not produced on account of this massive consumption of capital. The coming generation of Americans and countless others to come will be poorer by far as a result of our deficit spending.

"Of course, the beneficiaries of the redistribution process enjoy every moment of it. With men lacking vision, today's enjoyment is always more pleasurable than saving for tomorrow. In ignorance, they may applaud the very favors and handouts that are destroying their jobs and the wages they could have earned."

Mr. Sennholz explained the danger of bubbles. "Many failed to recognize the gradual development of financial bubbles especially in equity markets and real estate. Bubbles, which ultimately must deflate and come to naught, are difficult to spot because they closely resemble real economic expansion. Actually, they are visible symptoms of maladjustments caused by wanton money and credit creation and false interest rates. They enjoy the loud support and confirmation by the monetary authorities blowing the bubbles and by politicians who love the booms."

Mr. Sennholz made no bones about the final outcome. "The ultimate destination of the present road of political fiat is hyperinflation with all its ominous economic, social and political consequences."

CHAPTER 13

HOUSE OF CARDS

"Inflation is not a benign element in the economy's operation. It is, as it has always been, the most dangerous and destructive form of taxation."
Robert Higgs

Forty-two years ago I started Investment Rarities after reading a book called *Silver Profits in the Seventies*. Silver rose from $1.65 to $50. However, I never felt that silver had lived up to its promise. It should have been higher over the years. Most of the silver ever mined was used up by industry. The above ground supply was gone and yet the price languished.

I stuck with it through some mighty lean years because I had become a fervent believer that runaway inflation was inevitable. Today the bookstores are full of tomes warning about a pending crisis. Back then we had only a few publications every decade that suggested a coming crisis. However, we did have the books of the Austrian School economists, Mises, Hayek, Rothbard, Hazlitt, and Sennholz. These authors consistently forecast a bad ending for countries that resorted to inflating to pay their bills. Furthermore, they were death on government intervention, credit excess, high taxes, and socialism. They endorsed the market system and constructed the moral high ground on which capitalism rested.

However, forty-two years is a long time to preach about the inevitability of runaway inflation without it happening. Most assuredly we have experienced the booms and bust the Austrian School warns will accompany credit excess. Yet, the severe inflation that makes our financial affairs completely unmanageable remains at bay. Certainly we've had inflation. The dollar has lost 96% of its purchasing power in my lifetime. But we have been able to live with it. Now our bankers, politicians, and brokers wish to encourage inflation. In Washington and Wall Street inflation has gone from being our enemy to our friend and that is crazy. As economist Jörg Hülsmann points out, "Fiat inflation is a juggernaut of social, economic, cultural, and spiritual destruction." What he means is that inflation is how we pay for the welfare state and that makes the government bigger and the citizens worse off.

So what happened to the hyperinflation that was forecast over the years? We almost had it in 1979-1980 when interest rates were hiked to 19%. Then it became subdued despite the fact that the government kept on spending and financing its deficits with newly created money. We have been the chief inflationist in the world and it still hasn't caught up with us. One reason is that we started shipping money around the world to buy things. We exported our inflation for imports. We jacked up price inflation around the world while keeping it under control domestically.

Then the rest of the world caught on. They started printing money to pay for their spending just as did the U.S. So now we have the entire world inflating. Look at Japan and the European Union covering every dime the government spends (over what it takes in) with the printing press. China is experiencing its own 1929. Now it's not the U.S. alone that will crash and burn, it's the whole world.

The late economist Murray Rothbard told us what happens when inflation goes international: "At the end of the road will be a horrendous

NOW OUR BANKERS, POLITICIANS, AND BROKERS WISH TO ENCOURAGE INFLATION. IN WASHINGTON AND WALL STREET INFLATION HAS GONE FROM BEING OUR ENEMY TO OUR FRIEND AND THAT IS CRAZY.

worldwide hyperinflation, with no way of escaping into sounder or less inflated currencies."

When a nation embraces dishonesty as a policy and waters down its money it plants the seeds of financial destruction. What will come from the greatest monetary sin in history is the greatest economic punishment in history. You only have to think about it. $100 trillion in liabilities, $18 trillion in debt, trillions created each year to goose the economy, and $200 trillion created around the world. The more new money conjured up, the more that's needed. It can't go on much longer. None of it will be repaid. The cracks in the foundation are visible. This structure is coming down.

Central banks have trapped themselves. If they stop inflating, their economies crumble. They must forever apply greater doses of money and credit or face a depression. They cannot stop and they will not stop. That's why the public is seduced into believing that inflation is a good thing. Although it's a hidden tax that robs the citizenry of purchasing power, they've been taught to love it by the liberals in Washington and on Wall Street.

The fact that virtually everyone in America buys into the Keynesian argument that 2% inflation is good should make you a contrarian. Inflation has always been something to be avoided. Economic history proves that encouraging inflation is insanity. However, if you become a Keynesian contrarian, this can be a great environment for making money. Unfortunately, for most it will be a time of great losses. Those who buy the Keynesian argument will see their wealth destroyed as markets collapse and the currency is ruined. Prepare to see your institutions fail, your neighbors impoverished and your nation go bankrupt.

CHAPTER 14

A LITTLE PARANOIA IS GOOD

"Necessity is the plea for every infringement of human freedom. It is the argument of tyrants; it is the creed of slaves."
William Pitt

Reports of police standing aside or not showing up in Oakland to protect the public from unruly anti-Wall Street demonstrators should cause great alarm. When the police excuse themselves from their duty because of politics or because they are union members we are all at risk. These anti-Wall Street extremists share Lenin's revolutionary enthusiasm. He would murder anybody that got in his way. Some of these demonstrators are so full of hate and righteousness they too would justify atrocities against the rich. If the cops don't come when you call them it's the end of America as we've known it.

The Reds thought nothing of killing people to advance their cause. The Marxists made great use of criminals who joined the party and helped butcher the well-to-do, the entrepreneurs and those who had assets. They thought nothing of robbing the safe deposit boxes in every bank in Russia. How many of today's demonstrators are of similar ilk? Enough to make me slightly paranoid about our future safety and security.

These are Lenin's children. What the Marxists have done in the past they can do again. In Russia they hated the free market in agriculture. So they murdered 7 million farmers. They shot them, stabbed them, burned them and hung them. They took the mothers, children, babies and grandparents on trains to Siberia and dumped them off in winter with nothing but the clothes on their back. In spring not a soul could be found.

Richard Ebeling explains, "As many as 200 million people have died as part of the dream of creating a collectivist 'Paradise on Earth.' A 'new world' was taken to mean the mass murder of all those that the socialist revolutionary leaders declared to be 'class enemies,' including the families, the children of 'enemies of the people.'

41

"A witness wrote in 1920: 'The machine of the Red Terror works incessantly. Every day and every night, in Petrograd, Moscow, and all over the country the mountain of the dead grows higher. Everywhere people are shot, mutilated, wiped out of existence.'

"This murderous madness never ended. In the 1930's, during the time of the Great Purges instituted by Soviet dictator Josef Stalin to wipe out all 'enemies of revolution' through mass executions, there were also millions sent to the Gulag prisons that stretched across all of the Soviet Union to be worked to death as slave labor to 'build socialism.' Before being sent to their death or to the forced labor camps, tens of thousands would be interrogated and cruelly tortured to get confessions out of people about non-existent crimes, imaginary anti-Soviet conspiracies, and false accusations against others."

When the farmers resisted they were shot or deported to slave labor camps. Starvation became a policy. Vast areas were robbed of their grain. Food shipments were not allowed to go to the hungry. In 1933, 25,000 people died of starvation every day. It was written, "The once smiling young faces of children vanished forever amid the constant pain of hunger. It gnawed away at their bellies, which became grossly swollen, while their arms and legs became like sticks as they slowly starved to death." Three million children perished.

The farmers were obliterated. Meanwhile the *New York Times* claimed all talk of famine was ridiculous. The *Times* admired the Soviet system. Their reporter won the Pulitzer Prize for his glowing reports on Russia. These days the *Times* probably doesn't see anything wrong with the police letting a radical leftist mob and a bunch of union thugs destroy private property. What happens if the dollar fails and the money is no longer there for welfare, unemployment, food stamps and other social schemes? How big will the demonstrations be and how dangerous? Will the police and the National Guard be influenced by radical politicians and union bully boys? Will the criminals be unleashed on the 1%?

Igor Shafarevich, author and prisoner in the Gulag wrote: "Most socialist doctrines and movements are literally saturated with the mood of death, catastrophe, and destruction. One could regard the death of mankind as the final result to which the development of socialism leads."

It's important to remember how

ruthless and bloody socialists and statists have been. Nobody in Russia thought Lenin could prevail. The Czar and Czarina never dreamed that someday the Reds would herd their little family into a room and slaughter them. We have our share of collectivists and criminals in America who would do us harm. Backed by the "useful idiots" in the liberal party they could cause the ground beneath us to fall away. Keep this possibility in mind. If not for you, for your children and grandchildren. For them our fears should be ongoing. Our left wing political opponents are no strangers to a heritage of doing great evil in the name of good.

The writer Humberto Fontova recently wrote this about the *New York Times*' love affair with another murderous dictator: "The past 10 days have seen three hysterical editorials from the *New York Times* pleading for a U.S. economic lifeline to the Castro brothers to end the so-called embargo.

"In April of 1959 – amidst an appalling bloodbath of Cubans by firing squad ordered by Fidel Castro but mostly administered by his ever-faithful Igor, Che Guevara – Castro made a special visit to the *New York Times* offices in New York. After a warm greeting from Arthur Hayes Sulzberger, a beaming Fidel Castro personally decorated a beaming Herbert Matthews [who interviewed Castro for the *Times*] with a specially minted medal expressing his bloody regime's highest honor.

"'To our American friend Herbert Matthews with gratitude,' beamed Castro as the flashbulbs popped. 'Without your help, and without the help of the *New York Times*, the Revolution in Cuba would never have been.'"

"'Fidel Castro has strong ideas of liberty, democracy and social justice,' Matthews had written on the front pages of the world's most prestigious newspaper in February 1957. Reasonable people might ask: has any tiny little thing transpired in the intervening half-century that might cause the *New York Times* to regret their enabling of Fidel Castro?

"But reasonable people will search in utter vain for any hint of such regret, especially in light of recent editorials, which – if anything – double-down on the *Times*' historical fondness for the Castro regime. The *New York Times* enabled into power a regime that jailed and tortured political prisoners at a higher rate than Stalin's during the Great Terror."

CHAPTER 15

THE APPROACHING CALAMITY

"Never in our history have we been headed at such a breakneck speed toward our own financial, political and cultural destruction."
David Limbaugh

I wish my old friend Kurt Richebächer was still alive. He could analyze financial data like no other. His warnings about the future would resonate today. Kurt was born in Germany in 1918. He grew up in the Hitler era. Kurt came to Minneapolis in 1994 and stayed at my home for a few days. I questioned him about the war years in Germany. He was in the Wehrmacht. He completed basic training in 1941 and his unit was sent to the Russian front. A few days before they left he came down with a virus that paralyzed his legs. It might have been polio. He was hospitalized for months. His unit went to Russia and they were decimated. Most of his friends were killed. He told me that had he gone he never would have made it back to Germany.

After the war he returned to Berlin and earned a doctorate in economics. In 1964, he became chief economist and managing director of the Dresdner Bank. His rock ribbed stance on money and credit excess earned him the plaudits of Paul Volcker and John Exter. Sometime in the 1980's he moved to the south of France and began a monthly report called the Richebächer Letter. He was interviewed in a newsletter and when I read it I thought this guy thinks just like me. Believe me, at the time, kindred spirits were hard to find. I called him and introduced myself. Thereafter, we talked once or twice a month until he died in 2007 at age 89.

What would Kurt have to say about today's monetary shenanigans? In 1999 he wrote, "The U.S. financial system today hangs in an increasingly precarious position, a house of cards literally built on nothing but financial leverage, speculation and derivatives." Today he would be apoplectic. He would shout over the phone to me that our financial engineering and Federal Reserve debt monetization are economic sins that dwarf anything in the past.

As far back as 1996 he was warning about a stock market crash. "The bullish wave threatens to come crashing down on the hordes of analysts and investors who bet so heavily – and so foolishly – on their dreams of a perpetual 'stock market boom.'" As the Nasdaq bubble deflated he wrote in June of 2000, "The decisive cause of every single, serious economic and currency crisis are credit and debt excesses. Apparently, we cannot repeat it often enough: the U.S. credit and debt excesses of the past few years are beyond past experience in history, essentially leaving behind a totally vulnerable economy and financial system."

One of his sternest warnings came in 1999 when he criticized Alan Greenspan for his speech endorsing derivatives. "To be the leading central banker of the world, it really ought to be obvious that the overriding consequences of widespread derivatives use is excessive leverage and risk taking ... derivatives markets encourage a dangerous shifting of risk to parties with less wherewithal to shoulder potential losses. This is particularly the case during an acute financial crisis precisely when derivative 'insurance' is called for. We see ... massive shifting of market risk to the highly leveraged and exposed U.S. banking industry and Wall Street firms."

In 2002 he warned about the collapse of national savings: "The total carnage of national savings is the U.S. economy's most important – but also most widely ignored predicament ... national savings have been squandered to pay for spending that the consumer cannot afford from his current income."

He continued with a crucial economics lesson, one that the Keynesians have totally failed to grasp. "Ever since Adam Smith, savings has meant exactly one and the same thing in all languages: it is the part of current income that is not spent on consumption. And the key point of this definition is that such savings, and such savings only, make it possible to divert real resources from the production of consumption goods to the production of capital goods.

"To pin down and emphasize the key point: savings from current income represent the economy's supply of capital. Thus, it definitely sets the limits to the financial funds and the real resources that are available for new capital investment. Any increase in consumer spending as a share of GDP correspondingly decreases the economy's capacity for capital formation. It is, of course, easy to replace missing savings with credit creation. But there is no substitute for missing real resources.

"In the end it is all about capital investment. It is the critical mass in the process of economic growth that generates all the things that make for rising wealth and living standards. Capital investment creates demand, growing supply, employment, productivity, income, profits and tangible wealth."

He concluded, "The crucial thing to see about the U.S. economy is that its growth during the past few years was driven by uncontrolled debt creation for consumption and financial speculation, while in the process domestic savings and the potential for capital investment have been devastated as never before ... The first thing to get straight is that this was – and still is – the most outrageous bubble economy in history, far worse than the U.S. bubble of the 1920s and Japan's bubble of the late 1980s." (Remember, this was 2002.)

"Very few people so far have realized that the U.S. economy is sick to the bone. In the past few years it has been grossly mismanaged, on the macro level through unprecedented monetary looseness on the part of the Greenspan Fed, and on the micro level through corporate strategies that built only mountains of financial leveraging but no factories."

In 2005, he delivered this indictment of the U.S. economy. "The ongoing credit explosion is financing a lot of different things, except production and tangible capital formation. Debt growth is almost entirely used for unproductive purposes, such as consumption, imports, government deficits, purchases of existing assets and financial speculation."

He continued, "Credit growth in the United States has gone completely insane. This is sheer Ponzi financing – and like all Ponzi schemes someone will end up holding the bag. At the same time, the diversion of credit into bonds, stock and housing has created an illusion of bulging wealth.

"This so called wealth creation has its quack origins in loose money and artificially low interest rates; it boosts consumption at the expense of saving and investment. Strictly speaking, this is the exact opposite of wealth creation – impoverishment."

By 2006 Kurt Richebächer was warning about an impending

downturn. "The U.S. economy is in danger of a recession that will prove unusually severe and long ... The great question is what will happen to the variety of financial asset bubbles in the United States when the housing bubble bursts and the economy slumps."

In the spring of 2007 Kurt Richebächer suddenly lost his eyesight. In our last conversation I could hear the anguish in his voice as he explained to me that he had gone permanently blind. To someone who spent much of their time reading financial reports and economic statistics this was devastating beyond measure. Soon afterwards Kurt Richebächer passed away.

In one of his final newsletters in January of 2007 he wrote with amazing prescience, "In our view, the obvious major risk is in the impending bust of the gigantic housing bubble. Home ownership is broadly spread among the population, in contrast to owning stocks. So the breaking of the housing bubble will hurt the American people far more than did the collapse in stock prices in 2000 – 2002 ... Someday, the same will happen to the bond and stock market ... Another big risk is the dollar."

It's sad that Kurt Richebächer did not live to see the sorry outcome of the monetary excesses he warned about. The accuracy of his predictions makes him the soothsayer of the century. The economist Paul Krugman argued in 2002 that the Federal Reserve should do what it could to create a housing bubble; yet, he received a Nobel Prize. Nobody paid much attention to Kurt Richebächer and his accurate forecasts. In a rational world Kurt Richebächer would have won the Nobel and Krugman would have been fired.

Were he alive I'm sure Kurt Richebächer would agree with my view that Paul Krugman, from his influential post at the *New York Times* is the most dangerous and wrong-thinking economist since Karl Marx. Kurt would also have pilloried Mr. Bernanke and Janet Yellen just as he did Mr. Greenspan. He would argue that the politicians and monetary authorities in charge today suffer a profound economic ignorance. He would agree, they are leading us into catastrophe. He would be warning us about a falling dollar, a bursting bond bubble, a gathering recession and wrong-headed policy prescriptions coming from Washington. He would agree we could not be in worse hands.

CHAPTER 16

BREAD AND CIRCUSES

"Everyone wants to live at the expense of the State. They forget that the State lives at the expense of everyone."
Frédéric Bastiat

A few years ago I was fortunate enough to visit Rome and stand in the ruins of the Forum. Nothing else quite conveys the grandeur and greatness of Roman civilization. A new book, *The Rise of Rome*, explains the reasons for this success. It's the same reason the U.S. grew great – "favorable conditions for production and trade." The market economy, with its trade and commerce built Rome.

To explain the downfall of the Roman Empire, I rely on the famous historians Will and Ariel Durant. "To support officialdom – the army, the court, public works, and the dole – taxation rose to such heights that men lost incentive to work or earn, and an erosive contest began between lawyers finding devices to evade taxes and lawyers formulating laws to prevent evasion. Thousands of Romans, to escape the tax gatherer, fled over the frontiers to seek refuge among the barbarians."

Doesn't that sound familiar? The same high taxes, big government and excessive regulation that destroyed a once prosperous Roman civilization are in the process of doing the same thing here. Rome began to penalize the successful with smothering taxation and reward the unproductive with a dole (free bread and entertainment).

Eventually under the Emperor Diocletian in 301 AD, Rome fully embraced socialism. The bureaucrats feathered their own nest just as today's unionized government employees have established higher wages and superior benefits for themselves. Under socialism Roman civilization withered and died.

Ludwig von Mises explains why Rome failed and why we are failing. "Socialism is not in the least what it pretends to be. It is not the pioneer of a better and finer world, but the spoiler of what thousands of years of civilization have created. It does not build; it destroys. For destruction is the essence of it. It produces nothing, it only consumes what the social order based on private ownership in the means of production has created."

Mises went on to explain what happens to a civilization that embraces government intervention and socialism. "A society that chooses between capitalism and socialism does not choose between two social systems; it chooses between social cooperation and the disintegration of society. Socialism is not an alternative to capitalism; it is an alternative to any system under which men can live as human beings."

If this frightens you then well it should. We are nearly at the point where the welfare recipients and the subsidized are in control of who wins our elections. That means more government spending and higher taxes until the capitalist and entrepreneurs have been liquidated. Unfortunately, limitless borrowing is impossible and the markets will begin to abuse the dollar. As the value of the currency diminishes in the face of an inflationary holocaust the government will resort to even more socialism. Historians will write about the reasons for the decline and fall of America as they do about Rome. Basically Rome disappeared as a viable city. Its population shriveled. With our huge population of subsidized citizens (many of low character) there will be safer places in the world.

How do you and your loved ones negotiate the coming events? Paper money is rotting and one common prescription to offset its demise is to buy gold. We demure somewhat. A better prescription is to own silver. There's much less of it above ground. It has far more industrial demand and expanded uses. Furthermore it has a massive short position in the paper futures market, which must eventually be reckoned with and should gloriously impact the price.

It should be clear to any observer that we are moving in dramatic fashion away from the things that made us great – limited government, low taxes, free markets, and a rugged individualism that spurned the dole. We cannot survive socialism with any semblance of American greatness. No country has ever prospered for long with government intervention in the economy. The U.S. with its deficits and runaway government spending is doing a financial high wire act. By embracing more central bank inflation and other socialist schemes we ensure a terrible fall to the sawdust floor below. The Romans never saw their collapse coming. Most Americans are equally clueless. Nothing is so blind as the citizenry of a civilization in decline. However, once you suspect what is going to happen you can prepare and ready yourself. Factor our warnings into your thinking. So it is written, so it shall be.

CHAPTER 17

PARENTS OF THE YEAR

"The only way to break the cycle of unwed motherhood, fatherless children, poverty, crime, and welfare is to recognize that welfare causes more problems than it cures."
David Boaz

We condensed a recent news article in the Minneapolis newspaper:

"Multiple children were drinking alcohol and some were reportedly smoking marijuana in the house where a 3-year-old girl was found Monday night with a 0.12 percent blood-alcohol level. The children's mothers are sisters, age 32 and 31, each have six children ranging from 1 to 15. The petitions in juvenile court describe a chaotic scene where police found the toddler unresponsive, 'fresh vomit all over the house' and drunken adults yelling to each other.

"The 3-year-old drank Windsor Canadian whisky after the girl's 14-year-old brother gave it to her in a cup and said it was juice, court documents said. A 5-year-old daughter told authorities that she and three cousins, two of whom are 4 and 6, also drank alcohol. According to court documents: Police officers noticed a 'thick haze of smoke' and a strong smell of marijuana in the home. Children were smoking marijuana. Officers also found liquor spilled on the floor and soiled clothes and food strewn about the house. The 3-year-old's eyes were wide open but were glazed over and she was unresponsive.

"Officers found a juvenile male who appeared intoxicated and smelled strongly of alcohol crawling out a window. Adults home at the time – police have said there were four – were drunk and unable to dress the children. One mother was previously convicted of second-degree murder in 1997 and sentenced to five years in prison in the stabbing death of a woman. She has been the subject of five child-protection reports dating to 2000, including a finding of sexual abuse and endangerment regarding one of her daughters. The other mother's record includes theft convictions. She had multiple contacts with County Child Protection, most stemming from domestic assaults."

If you think preschoolers smoking marijuana are a rarity, you're wrong. It's not uncommon among the urban underclass. That says nothing about sexual promiscuity, thievery, drug peddling and violence among pre-teens and young adults. It's a social mess of staggering proportions brought to you by our liberal social thinkers and bureaucrats. Social agencies are so incompetent they will not remove an innocent child or even a tiny infant from abusive, chemically dependent mothers with scumbag boyfriends. Sexual and physical abuse goes unnoticed and ignored. These brutes are killing infants and children accidentally or on purpose with alarming frequency. Unfortunately, little kids who survive these toxic mothers, relatives and boyfriends are likely to grow up to be hoodlums themselves. This is the circle of dependency and crime that government is purchasing for you with your own money. Your tax dollars fund social programs that produce grossly dysfunctional criminals and addicts. Unfortunately, your grandchildren face the prospect of life among swelling numbers of remorseless criminals.

Our cities are full of similar horror stories. Social programs that pay unwed mothers for every child they have only encourages the least responsible to have multiple births. By some estimates, the birth rate of the underclass is three times greater than that of the general population. There are a million little kids in our country whose character is being ruined by lack of love, chaotic behavior and bad example. Alcoholics, drug addicts, prostitutes and criminals are not fit to raise children. Social workers should be tarred and feathered for leaving babies with these lowlifes. If you took these infants away from the clowns raising them and put them in good homes, twenty years from now they'd be graduating from college instead of going to prison.

We're worrying about the wrong things in this country. What could be more important than protecting little children from criminally negligent adults? What could be more important than transferring kids from behavioral hellholes into loving, secure homes or even orphanages? Prohibitions against interracial adoptions are the insane handiwork of liberal social workers. The American people will step up and save these children if given a chance. For that to happen, the liberals must see the gravity of the problem and admit their policies have caused this social mayhem. Frankly, I think they would

OUR CITIES ARE FULL OF SIMILAR HORROR STORIES. SOCIAL PROGRAMS THAT PAY UNWED MOTHERS FOR EVERY CHILD THEY HAVE ONLY ENCOURAGES THE LEAST RESPONSIBLE TO HAVE MULTIPLE BIRTHS.

rather turn their back on these kids than admit their socialist claptrap is bankrupt.

Child welfare workers are mostly liberal. They often push to have abused and endangered children reunited with their worthless parents. For example, a Minneapolis mother convicted of prostitution, drug crimes and other offenses who lost rights to two children due to frequent maltreatment was reunited with her two-year old son by order of the county.

As a newborn the baby tested positive for high levels of opiates and cocaine. Foster parents weaned him off the drug with methadone as he cried in pain. Nevertheless, the infant was sent back to his mother. When presented with evidence of the mother's continued drug use and prostitution, the county refused to intervene. Recently, the mother was advertising her availability as a prostitute and had the boy with her when she was arrested with four others in a hotel room strewn with dirty needles, crack pipes, cocaine and meth. The boy was then passed around to four or five people and the county lost track of him. Eventually the father was arrested for an unrelated crime and directed police to relatives who had the boy. Hopefully, the foster parents who want to adopt him will get the boy back. Believe it or not the court may still return him to his mother.

When you multiply stories like this thousands of times you get a sense of how much behavioral damage liberal social policies cause. Criminals and addicts who should never raise a child are given this responsibility time and again by social workers and the courts. If you wanted to raise a crop of hoodlums and gangsters this is how you do it. Chalk another massive failure up to liberalism.

CHAPTER 18

LIBERAL ENVY

"Under the influence of collectivist ideologies, many politicians and journalists are ever eager to strike at successful entrepreneurs who earn much more than they do. It is difficult to ascertain their motives; it can be simple envy which consumes many men, or it can be economic ignorance."
Hans F. Sennholz

I have these two acquaintances who are big believers in high taxes and heavy government regulation. One is a lawyer who did OK in his career but never made a lot of money. The other was in real estate and after years of disappointing results retired with modest means. They are both envious of people who made a lot of money. Envy is what makes them liberals.

Scratch a leftist and you'll find a person who's worried about someone else making a profit or high income. Why is that? Envy explains these sentiments. Author Helmut Schoeck writes, "Envy is a drive which lies at the core of man's life as a social being ..." In America the politics of envy can get you elected to the highest office in the land.

Under capitalism, everyone has the opportunity to become an entrepreneur or attain a profession or position that pays off handsomely. However, this system allows no excuses for personal shortcomings or failures. Many self-made people started from the same place as others who failed or who did not forge ahead. The sight of people who have given proof of greater ability bothers some people. To console themselves they rationalize that their skills have gone unrecognized. They blame capitalism, which they claim does not reward the meritorious but gives the prize to dishonest businesses, and other exploiters. They were too honest to swindle people, and they chose virtue over riches.

In a society where everyone is the founder of his or her own fortune, it is particularly galling to the teacher, the politician, the artist or the bureaucrat to see the large income disparity between themselves and successful entrepreneurs. Their envy turns them to socialism, which promises to level incomes and allows the state to control economic outcomes.

Ludwig von Mises put it this way: "Envy is a widespread frailty. It is certain that many intellectuals envy the higher income of prosperous businessmen and that these feelings drive them toward socialism. They believe that the authorities of a socialist commonwealth would pay them higher salaries than those that they earn under capitalism." Mises further argued, "What pushes the masses into the camp of socialism is even more than the illusion that socialism will make them richer, the expectation that it will curb all those who are better than they themselves are ..."

Even among some conservatives there exists an unhealthy level of envy toward the wealthy. They join with professors and politicians to suggest that the worst exploitation and greed comes from big business. They fail to realize that large corporations got that way because they did a superior job of meeting the product needs of the people in the best, most economical way. The hallmark of big business is mass production for the benefit of the masses. Big business standardizes the people's ways of consumption and enjoyment, and every citizen shares in most of these material blessings.

As for Wall Street, the current fiasco exemplifies pigging out at the government banquet table. When the government grants subsidies or provides cheap loans abuses are inevitable. When the government guarantees financial assets and removes risk, excesses are bound to occur. When the government keeps interest rates artificially low and money and credit loose speculators and risk takers push the envelope. When the regulators fail as they usually do, abuses occur and tremendous losses are inflicted on gullible investors who think that regulation protects them. Furthermore, the excesses of Wall Street hardly personify the vast number of businesses that are truly representative of capitalism.

Nobody goes without in the market economy because someone got rich. The same process that makes people rich satisfies people's wants and needs. The most millionaires are found in countries with the highest living standards. The entrepreneurs and the capitalists prosper only to the extent that they succeed in supplying and satisfying consumers. The glaring misunderstanding of capitalism and how it works in our society originates more from envy than intellect. This mix of envy and ignorance explains the inroads of socialists who have led us down the path to fewer freedoms and more government.

CHAPTER 19

EXPROPRIATE THE CAPITALISTS

"Capitalism denies the right of government to take the property of a private citizen at will, or to tax away his livelihood at will, or to tell him when and where he must work or how and where he must live. Capitalism is built in the firm foundation of individual liberty."
Perry Gresham

Columnist Vasko Kohlmayer quoted Michael Moore in Moore's film, *Capitalism: A Love Story*. "Capitalism is an evil, and you cannot regulate evil ... you have to eliminate it and replace it with something that is good for all people." Kohlmayer disagrees: "Capitalism is increasingly cast as the great villain of our time. It's blamed for exploitation, poverty, fraud, alienation, crime, racism and nearly everything else.

"The bad rap could not be more undeserved. Rather than mankind's scourge, capitalism has been its greatest benefactor. It is, in fact, the only socio-economic system that can provide ordinary people with dignified and prosperous lives.

It was only with the advent of capitalism that the common man was able to escape the penury and filth of his existence to which he had been previously consigned. Until then, the lives of most people were short, hard and miserable. Today, as if by miracle, we can enjoy greater comforts and ease of life than the kings of the past."

Author Lew Rockwell confirms, "Capitalism, and capitalism alone, has rescued the human race from degrading poverty, rampant sickness and early death."

Kohlmayer points out, "Capitalism is responsible for nearly everything that makes human existence easy and comfortable. The automobile, the supermarket, the personal computer, the washing machine, the hammer-drill, the iPhone, the airplane, the TV set, the chewing gum, electricity and countless other good things have all been birthed and mass produced by capitalism."

Rockwell agrees. "The profit

system balances human needs with the availability of all the world's resources, unleashes the amazing power of human creativity, and works to meet the material needs of every member of society at the least possible cost. It does this through exchange, cooperation, competition, entrepreneurship, and all the institutions that make possible capitalism – the most productive economic system this side of heaven."

Says Kohlmayer, "Because of its immense wealth-generating power, people who live in capitalist societies enjoy rising standards of living and material affluence. Conversely, those who live in non-capitalist societies invariably experience the opposite ... The rule always holds: Capitalist societies are invariably prosperous. Non-capitalist ones are always poor."

Columnist Walter Williams sums it up; "Not withstanding all of the demagoguery, it is capitalism not socialism that made us a great country and it's socialism that will be our undoing."

What's going on with Michael Moore and the Hollywood left? Actors like Sean Penn and Danny Glover were kissing up to the late socialist dictator Chavez in Venezuela. They seem to prefer a government strong man who will confiscate the property and wealth of those who earned it and transfer it to illiterates in exchange for their votes. This

CAPITALISM IS INCREASINGLY CAST AS THE GREAT VILLAIN OF OUR TIME. IT'S BLAMED FOR EXPLOITATION, POVERTY, FRAUD, ALIENATION, CRIME, RACISM AND NEARLY EVERYTHING ELSE.

must also be their vision for America. These are dangerous trends. If they were to prevail, those of us who aim to prosper will be on the outside looking in. Capitalists may even become like the Russian kulaks (farmers) who were exterminated by Stalin in order to implement collective farming. A liberal hero Che Guevara advised, "the oppressors must be killed mercilessly ... the revolutionary must become an efficient and selective killing machine."

Michael Moore has a lot more in common with the Bolsheviks than anyone would like to think. The author David Horowitz (a former associate of the Black Panthers who experienced the Panthers' murder of a friend) has become the leading authority on the radical left.

He puts it this way: "It's interesting that we have words

like 'neo-Nazi' to describe post-Hitler Nazis, and 'neo-conservative' to describe liberals who left the Democratic Party when it took a sharp turn to the left, but not 'neo-Communist' to describe the massive numbers of people on the left – and among them very influential people – who share, almost to the jot and title, the old communist view of capitalism, and are prepared to act on that perception ... Neo-communists like Moore share the old communists' antipathy for the United States and sympathy for its enemies, even enemies as evil as Iran and Hezbollah.

"A neo-communist is someone who is convinced that race, class, and gender hierarchies make it not only legitimate but necessary to describe America as a 'white supremacist' society. Neo-communists believe that a revolution is necessary (if not opportune at the moment), that the Constitution is a disposable document, and that America's communist and Islamo-fascist enemies (Iran, Venezuela, Cuba, Nicaragua, Hezbollah, the PLO and Hamas) are freedom fighters or at least on the right side of the Armageddon that faces us.

"These are views shared by *The Nation* magazine, by Commonsense.org, by the Indymedia crowd, by the social justice movement, by the majority of the Black Caucus and the Progressive Caucus on the Democratic side in Congress and by tens of thousands of university professors who indoctrinate their students in these pernicious ideologies every day. They are the views held by the leaders of ACORN, the SEIU, AFCSME, and other leftwing unions, by radical feminists, by organizations like MALDEF and La Raza, by the ACLU and the Center for Constitutional Rights. This coalition, which I have called the 'unholy alliance,' presents a massive threat to America's security and its individual freedoms and its free market system."

> "CAPITALISM, AND CAPITALISM ALONE, HAS RESCUED THE HUMAN RACE FROM DEGRADING POVERTY, RAMPANT SICKNESS AND EARLY DEATH."
>
> – LEW ROCKWELL

CHAPTER 20

IGNORING RISK

"The proper and limited use of government is to invoke a common justice and keep the peace – and that is all."
Leonard Read

The other night my wife and I went to a housewarming. It was a large gathering of people, most of whom I didn't know. Always at a loss for much to say at such events, I mentioned to a couple of acquaintances the high degree of risk existent in the world today. One friend thought I meant the risk of getting mugged or having a traffic accident. The other asked if what I meant was risk in financial markets. One acknowledged that his stocks were down but didn't seem to see much risk. My goodness, I thought, how far from the mainstream must I be?

The acid test of intelligence is whether the things you believe in turn out to be true. Thus it's always good to periodically examine one's premises. The books of the Austrian School economists, Ludwig von Mises, Murray Rothbard and Nobel Prize winner Friedrich Hayek make me more certain than ever that we as a nation have drifted so far from rational economic moorings that a monumental financial disorder cannot be avoided.

Today, Austrian economics remains a little known economic school. Contemporary economists totally ignore the Austrian school and question the sanity of anyone who would use this obscure philosophy as the springboard for views that predict financial catastrophe. Nevertheless, Austrian school thinking, however unfashionable, has impressive intellectual credentials. For example, economists from Adam Smith to Karl Marx believed that the value of a thing was determined by the amount of labor that went into making it. Thus Marx could claim that since laborers created the value of things they were due all the profits and that capitalists were cheating them. "Workers of the world unite." From this premise spread the disruptive Marxist philosophy which at times seemed to own the world (especially intellectuals within the United States).

However, in Austria a professor of economics (Böhm-Bawerk)

developed a different explanation of how a thing got value. He knew that ten thousand men could labor to build a pyramid and no one would pay anything for it. But pick up a diamond off an Arkansas hillside and you could sell it for $10,000. Why was gold worth more than silver, which was more useful to industry? This was the paradox of value, which no economist could resolve.

Böhm-Bawerk knew that you and other consumers are the true arbiters of value. You choose whether an item has value to you. Value is subjective. If you have three wagonloads of grain to last you the winter and you plan to eat one load, use another for seed and feed the birds with the other, you would naturally price them differently. You would trade the third load for much less than the second. The last (or most recent) sale you make of a bag of grain from your wagon is the present value. It's called marginal utility. The bag of the least marginal utility (value to you) sets the value.

The Austrians solved the value paradox by stating that you don't value the entire world supply of an item, but only a given supply, which you can use at that moment. This brilliant analysis became the accepted economic alternative to the value theory of Marxist economists and the core of Austrian economic theory. Economics professor Hans Sennholz states that the Austrians "thereby managed to place the individual in the center of their analysis and the consumer at the core of the economic order."

Socialists want the state to determine price and value; the Austrians know that only the individual can accomplish this. The buying choices of the individual make the world go round and this free choice is basic to our liberty. The buying choice of the consumer determines profit and loss and the success and failure of businesses and products.

In the 1930's, the economic thought of John Maynard Keynes made an influential mark and relegated the Austrian school to the back of the bus. Among other things, Keynes pushed consumption over savings and government intervention over market solutions. The state manipulated taxes, money supply, government spending and subsidies to foster demand. The politicians loved it and today we are told, "We are all Keynesians." Were he alive today, John Maynard Keynes would cringe at our low savings, stock speculation and excessive monetary meddling. He would refuse to take any blame for such extremes.

Austrian economics bases its views on the actions of individuals. These actions can't be codified because of the unpredictable responses people will give to each circumstance. You prefer chewing gum while I like breath mints. You by a pack at a time, I go to Sam's and load up. Modern economics tends to treat us like so many units, with algebraic certainty. Economic outcomes cannot be determined by laws similar to physics. Austrian economics does not lend itself to mathematics. Professor Mises dismissed mathematical analysis as unworkable poppycock. Economics is a branch of philosophy and not an exercise of math. Yet, the most influential mathematical economist in the United States today does not recognize Austrian economics because it does not lend itself to mathematics.

Today we inflate at will. Fiat money created out of thin air, runaway government borrowing, huge government financial guarantees, staggering levels of leverage in securities markets, consumer credit excesses, negative savings rates, and monstrous trade and budget deficits have created a financial house of cards. Mises warned that the employment of these policies leads to economic disaster and makes a collapse inevitable. Mises is the economist whose views you should listen to. Not the Marxists and socialists of academia, not the Wall Street and Washington Keynesians who manipulate interest rates and money supply and claim to foster everlasting prosperity.

In my book, *The Start-Up Entrepreneur*, I quoted F. W. Woolworth, who claimed that Dutch businessmen of Puritan stock taught him how to flourish in business without borrowing money. Contrast the go-go world of today's easy money with the way things once were when gold was money. "They ran their stores on the same policy for more than half a century; they did not progress, except as a tree progresses in size. They grew wealthy slowly, but surely. They never went into debt: they always paid for what they bought, and paid with cash. They bought at the lowest price, and they bought not a cent's worth more than they actually needed. When they put money in the bank – salted it away – it was put away to stay. There were no liens on anything they owned. These Dutch farmers taught me to manage my own business and never to let my business manage me."

CHAPTER 21

WITHOUT MERIT

"Since the 8th Century in China, hundreds of fiat money monetary systems have been attempted. And 100% of the time, they have failed. Why should a monetary system, that hasn't worked for 1200 years, suddenly work now?"
Lawrence M. Parks

Almost forty years ago, I left a comfortable family business and went to Miami to start a drinking water company. This endeavor was a huge personal struggle, full of financial peril, rejection and anxiety. I devoted a chapter to this ordeal in my book, *The Start-Up Entrepreneur*. Fortunately, after more than a year of work and strain a wealthy family made me an offer I couldn't refuse and I sold out to them. For a few months after that I was in the chips.

I returned to Minnesota and with a partner started Investment Rarities. In two years (1975) our money was gone and we were on the ropes. One crisis led to another. At a critical moment my partner buckled. He proclaimed our venture was defunct and tried to leave with one of our few potential assets. We had a falling out. I bought his stock for very little. He left me with a load of debt and unpaid bills.

At the moment we stared failure in the face he quit while I persisted. He had no faith in our future while I was sure we would ultimately succeed. Why? I had an enormous advantage over him. I had previously suffered through the despair and pain of near failure in my water business. This had strengthened me. My partner lacked persistence because he had no prior experience with struggle. In his previous enterprise he had made a lot of money without paying much of a price. Things had been easier for him.

The founder of U.S. Steel, Andrew Carnegie, strived for success in business so that he "should never again be called upon to endure such nights and days of racking anxiety." I have suffered through these severe business droughts and cyclical downturns over the past four decades and one thing stands out. The struggles of life teach the truly valuable lessons. We learn little from good times and virtually nothing from success. Emerson said it best. "When man [or woman] ... is pushed, tormented, defeated, he has a chance to learn something; he has been put on his wits, on his manhood, he has gained facts, learns his ignorance, is cured of the insanity of conceit; has got moderation and real skill."

Now suppose that at the inception of my Miami water business there was a government program for young men that awarded me a large contract. My life would have been so much easier. I would have been an immediate success. At first glance this would have helped me enormously, but in reality it would have crippled me. I would have missed the lessons and struggles that had made me resourceful. Every bout of pain in life makes the next round more likely to be endured.

The government has programs and requirements that give money, or business contracts to women and minorities. These preferences supposedly help the recipient. But they do not. They simply relieve these people from learning the necessary lessons required to climb to the top and succeed on merit.

Those who oppose these government preferences are thought to be mean-spirited or reactionary. The media brands

> **THE STRUGGLES OF LIFE TEACH THE TRULY VALUABLE LESSONS. WE LEARN LITTLE FROM GOOD TIMES AND VIRTUALLY NOTHING FROM SUCCESS.**

them as chauvinists or racists. In reality, most business owners or managers want a level playing field and would like to see minorities and women reach the upper levels of achievement. Most men in business want all people to experience success and are not in the least threatened by this prospect. But those of us who have struggled time and again know that this can never be accomplished with shortcuts. The government's subsidy programs will ruin the chances of minorities and women to take their place on the pinnacles of success. If you accept business contracts or money you didn't earn to speed your success, you undermine your long-term prospects and incur the dead opposite of what the government strives to accomplish.

If you get a job or promotion because of your race or gender, it is no different than a subsidy. You get something that you didn't earn, something for nothing. You are weaker for it than if you climbed the ladder by yourself. It may seem like a helping hand, but if it deprives you of skill and inner strength it is a push backwards. Nothing good ever comes from getting something you didn't earn.

Now the government and the media encourage those who get entitlements to see themselves as victims. This is just one more horribly negative outcome of subsidies. Once trapped in the belief that you are a victim, you surrender your birthright to compete for the prizes of life. In the mind of the victims and their sponsors, everything controversial that happens in the country becomes just another result and a plot to keep them from succeeding. Such perceptions inevitably become reality.

It's not just the underclass that suffers from something for nothing. A corollary exists with the children of wealthy people who shield their offspring from economic struggle. If you are affluent and want to harm your children, give them all the money they will ever need. If you leave them your fortune before they've made their own way, they will be weaker for it. Rich or poor, insulate youngsters from life's struggles and you will fashion people who cannot stand on their own, cannot build, accomplish or create.

Herein lies the principle threat to American freedom, prosperity and greatness. Napoleon Hill said it best, "When a majority of the people of any nation give up their inherited prerogative right to make their own way through struggle, history shows clearly that the entire nation is in a tailspin of decay that inevitably must end in extinction."

CHAPTER 22

THE KEYNESIAN FALLACY

> *"The unprecedented success of Keynesianism is due to the fact that it provides an apparent justification for the 'deficit spending' policies of contemporary governments. It is the pseudo-philosophy of those who can think of nothing else than to dissipate the capital accumulated by previous generations."*
> **Ludwig von Mises**

Here's a quote from PayPal founder Peter Thiel's excellent book *Zero to One*: "If you can identify a delusional popular belief, you can find what lies behind it: the contrarian truth." We are confronted daily with the greatest economic and financial delusion of all time: Keynesian economics. The contrarian truth behind Keynesianism is that it must fail. Government is the greatest advocate of Keynesian economics because it finances government spending. The socialism that's paid for by Keynesian money creation has never worked in history, but has engineered economic and social suffering on a scale so enormous we can't comprehend it.

Besides socialism, the other great beneficiary of Keynesian policies is Wall Street and its minions who see no harm as long as stocks finish up. They care not about the loss to the public's savings or the income disparity that inflation creates. These shallowest of thinkers ignore the speculative excess and the inevitable boom and bust to worship at the altar of the Fed. They fail to understand that the money printing they swoon over is the favored method of financing the welfare state and socialism.

The essence of Keynesianism in America is money creation and inflation. In his book *The Ethics of Money Production*, the Austrian economist Jörg Hülsmann described inflation's cultural and spiritual legacy: "The notion that inflation is harmful is a staple of economic science. To appreciate the disruptive nature of inflation in its full extent we must keep in mind that it springs from a

64

violation of the fundamental rules of society. Inflation is what happens when people increase the money supply by fraud, imposition, and breach of contract. Invariably it produces three characteristic consequences: (1) it benefits the perpetrators at the expense of all other money users; (2) it allows the accumulation of debt beyond the level debts could reach on the free market; and (3) it reduces the purchasing power of money below the level it would have reached on the free market.

"While these three consequences are bad enough, things get much worse once inflation is encouraged and promoted by the state. The government's fiat makes inflation perennial, and as a result we observe the formation of inflation-specific institutions and habits. Thus fiat inflation leaves a characteristic cultural and spiritual stain on human society."

More important for the short term are the economic consequences, which include the possible destruction of the dollar through hyperinflation. This inevitable outcome is brought on by our ongoing monetization of the debt. You cannot pay a nation's bills forever by printing or creating new money. The markets will eventually enforce repercussions. No money in history has withstood permanent inflating. In fact, all paper, fiat currencies have become worthless for the same reason.

No one ever explained the damage that inflation does like the great Libertarian writer for *Newsweek* and the *New York Times*, Henry Hazlitt (1894 – 1993). He wrote, "When the Federal Reserve banks buy government notes or bonds in the open market, they pay for them, directly or indirectly, by creating money. This is what is known as 'monetizing' the public debt. Inflation goes on as long as this goes on." The consequences are dire indeed. "Inflation must always end in a crisis and a slump, and worse than the slump itself may be the public delusion that the slump has been caused, not by the previous inflating, but by the inherent defects of a free market."

Hazlitt warned, "It is harmful because it depreciates the value of the monetary unit, raises everybody's cost of living, imposes what is in effect a tax on the poorest... wipes out the value of past savings, discourages future savings, redistributes wealth and income wantonly, encourages and rewards speculation and gambling at the expense of thrift and work, undermines confidence in the justice of a free enterprise system, and corrupts public and private morals."

He continued, "A period of inflation is almost inevitably also a period when demagogy and antibusiness mentality are rampant. If implacable enemies of the country had deliberately set out to undermine and destroy the incentives of the middle classes to work and save, they could hardly have contrived a more effective set of weapons than the present combination of inflation, subsidies, handouts, and confiscatory taxes that our own politicians have imposed upon us."

Mr. Hazlitt explained further, "In a free enterprise system, with an honest and stable money, there is dominantly a close link between effort and productivity on the one hand, and economic reward on the other. Inflation severs this link. Reward comes to depend less and less on effort and production, and more and more on successful gambling and luck."

He continued his litany of warnings: "It is not merely that inflation breeds dishonesty in a nation. Inflation is itself a dishonest act on the part of government, and sets the example for private citizens. When modern governments inflate by increasing the paper money supply, directly or indirectly, they do in principle what kings once did when they clipped coins. Diluting the money supply with paper is the moral equivalent of diluting the milk supply with water. Notwithstanding all the pious pretenses of governments that inflation is some evil visitation from without, inflation is practically always the result of deliberate governmental policy."

WE ARE CONFRONTED DAILY WITH THE GREATEST ECONOMIC AND FINANCIAL DELUSION OF ALL TIME: KEYNESIAN ECONOMICS. THE CONTRARIAN TRUTH BEHIND KEYNESIANISM IS THAT IT MUST FAIL.

In 1931 Mr. Bresciani-Turroni wrote of the Weimar inflation in Germany, "It annihilated thrift … it destroyed incalculable moral and intellectual values. It provoked a serious revolution in social classes, a few people accumulating wealth and forming a class of usurpers of national property, whilst millions of individuals were thrown into poverty. It was a distressing preoccupation and constant torment of innumerable families; it poisoned the German people by spreading among all classes the spirit of speculation and by diverting them from proper and regular work, and it was the cause of incessant political and moral disturbances." That was in 1931, before the hell that followed.

In 1876 Andrew Dickson White wrote of the great French inflation of the 1790's, "With prices soaring and the value of money savings rapidly diminishing, an early effect was the obliteration of thrift. Accompanying this was a cancerous increase in speculation and gambling. Stockjobbing became rife. More and more people began to see the advantages of borrowing and later paying off in depreciated money. A great debtor class grew up whose interest was to keep the inflation going. Workers, finding themselves with less and less real pay in terms of what their wages would buy, while others grew rich by gambling, began to lose interest in steady work. The evaporation of the incomes and savings of the lower and middle classes, and the sudden enrichment of speculators, with their ostentatious luxury, led to mounting social resentment and unrest."

Periods of inflation in the modern era are often interspersed with periods of deflation. That's because money and credit creation generate a boom in the economy which ultimately leads to a bust. Sometimes the newly created money fails to stoke a booming economy, but flows into assets. When stocks and real estate increase dramatically in a period of easy money that is asset inflation. A period of deflation can lead to bear markets and declining asset values.

Deflation is both good and bad. When oil prices plunge, consumers pay less for gasoline. Meanwhile, oil companies with high level of debt must file for bankruptcy when they can't service their debt. When commodities deflate, major mining companies and other corporations are at risk. With 200 trillion of the debt in the world, deflation can erode the value of the underlying collateral that supports these loans. This would set off cascading bankruptcies. Central Banks would be throwing money out of helicopters before that happens. Inflating is baked into the cake until the dollar and other paper currencies have lost so much value they are no longer trusted.

CHAPTER 23

THE ENEMY WITHIN

"What the political left, even in democratic countries, share is the notion that knowledgeable and virtuous people like themselves have both a right and a duty to use the power of government to impose their superior knowledge and virtue on others." **Thomas Sowell**

Nobody gets under the skin of conservatives and libertarians like Paul Krugman, columnist for the *New York Times*. Lately he's sunk to a new low by claiming that the underlying motivation for conservative views is racial. He wrote, "Race is the Rosetta Stone that makes sense ... of U.S. politics." He claims that conservative politics is driven by the belief that liberals are taking their hard earned money and giving it to minorities.

Arguments like this further drive a wedge between the races and the two political parties. It's more than divisive, it's hateful. The reality is that conservatives want to see minorities succeed. For the most part they bend over backwards to help people.

Conservatives are known to be far more charitable than liberals. They are not in the least threatened by the success of anyone.

However, conservatives do understand one exceedingly important thing. People must make their own way in life. The helping hand of the government is too often a push backwards. When permanent subsidies began to replace private charity, the circumstances of the poor took a turn for the worse and their condition continues to deteriorate to this day.

Nothing differentiates the views of the left and right like this sentence by Mr. Krugman: "The reason so many Americans remain trapped in poverty isn't that the government helps them too much; it's that it helps them too little." The trillions spent on social welfare have left wide swaths of people unemployable and unable to fend for themselves. Crime and addiction have worsened. Unwed mothers and irresponsible parents have doomed untold numbers of children to the criminal justice system. Underprivileged people were far more upright a century ago, before subsidies.

The failure to see the cause of society's disintegration and the threat it poses for America makes Mr. Krugman's errors the modern equivalent of a belief in human sacrifice. Furthermore, his Keynesian economic theories have caused inflation and the housing bubble. In fact, he recommended the creation of a housing bubble prior to the housing collapse that caused

However, conservatives do understand one exceedingly important thing. People must make their own way in life. The helping hand of the government is too often a push backwards.

untold pain for homeowners. His endorsement of deficit spending, excessive regulation and exorbitant taxes are policies that have hamstrung the economy. Nevertheless, he does the thinking for a vast contingent of liberals from his influential post at the *Times*.

Many on the left are in awe of Nobel Prize winning Krugman. However, when you read some of the things he has written the genius label doesn't apply. Here's what Krugman said about the Internet and technology back in 1998: "The growth of the Internet will slow drastically, as the flaw in 'Metcalfe's law,' which states that the number of potential connections in a network is proportional to the square of the number of participants, becomes apparent: most people have nothing to say to each other! By 2005 or so, it will become clear that the Internet's impact on the economy has been no greater than the fax machine .... As the rate of technological change in computing slows, the number of jobs for IT specialists will decelerate, then actually turn down; ten years from now, the phrase 'information economy' will sound silly."

CHAPTER 24

EGALITARIAN NONSENSE

"The current veneration of equality is, indeed, a very recent notion in the history of human thought. Among philosophers or prominent thinkers the idea scarcely existed before the mid-eighteenth century; if mentioned, it was only as the object of horror or ridicule."
Murray Rothbard

Liberals at the U.S. Securities and Exchange Commission recently approved a rule requiring all companies to disclose the pay gap between the chief executive and the typical worker. This gives a new weapon to groups protesting income inequality. Compliance with this new rule is an added expense for business. Companies will have to disclose the median compensation of all employees and publish a ratio comparing it to the bosses' pay.

All this springs from a collectivist mentality. Why is it okay for a basketball player to make $25 million a year or a singer to make $100 million while a CEO who has run a profitable company with 130,000 employees gets accused of greed? This policy could be a first step in trying to limit the compensation of business leaders. It makes as much sense to compare what LeBron James makes with the incomes of the fans who pay to watch him. Beyoncé made $115 million last year. How does that compare with the incomes of those who attended her concerts?

The contribution to the public well being by the major corporations who provide our goods and services dwarfs the contribution of actors, athletes and entertainers. This attack on CEO pay by liberals and socialists is an attempt to control all businesses and redistribute profits and incomes.

In the world's poorest countries such as Bangladesh, there are virtually no millionaires. In impoverished African nations, wealthy Africans hardly exist. In countries with the most billionaires, living standards are highest and countries with the most new millionaires have the greatest number of people escaping poverty. In other words, when the entrepreneurs of a nation prosper and create wealth, it benefits all the people. Furthermore, when they plow back their earnings to expand their businesses or finance a new business, it grows the wealth of a country even more.

So why do the world's dumbest people want to take away the money that successful people earn? They think it's unfair for someone to make too much. However, people like Steve Jobs make fortunes because of breakthroughs that change the world. Those rewards are justified. Big incomes accrue to people who provide superior goods and services that people want. They create jobs and raise living standards, and if they have a lot more money than someone camping under a bridge, isn't that the way it should be?

Inequality also spurs people on. They want more in life so they strive to reach the upper levels of their occupations. Inequality gives all of us examples of what to shoot for. We want what successful people have. Inequality acts as an incentive.

I once wrote about an island in Florida populated by wealthy people. Each day, hundreds of trades-people cross the bridge to work for the affluent residents. Housekeepers, electricians, landscapers, painters, exterminators, and maintenance people are just a few of those who are employed by the rich. Affluent people create jobs with their money.

A foolish economist like the Frenchman Thomas Piketty, whose book the liberals are swooning over, wants to take away everyone's wealth. Apparently his plan for the money is to give the government more. That sounds more like a plan to exterminate civilization. France is a nation on the verge of ruin through following the advice of socialists like Piketty.

Capitalists also give their wealth away to worthwhile causes. Think of Gates in Africa or Sloan and Kettering or the huge gifts from the wealthy to museums, charities, colleges and hospitals. Rich people do good things for society.

The left believes that if one person gets rich it takes away from others. They aren't smart enough to see that if that were true, we could not progress. Capitalism is about giving before receiving and creating new wealth that underlies rising living standards. Impractical leftists who know nothing about economics or business went to implement policies that will make us all poor. They must be stopped.

THE LEFT BELIEVES THAT IF ONE PERSON GETS RICH IT TAKES AWAY FROM OTHERS. THEY AREN'T SMART ENOUGH TO SEE THAT IF THAT WERE TRUE, WE COULD NOT PROGRESS.

The author Llewellyn Rockwell, Jr. tells us, "We are told how terrible it is that some people should have so much more than others, but rarely if ever are we told how much (if any) extra wealth the egalitarian society would allow the better-off to have.

"The reason the state holds up equality as a moral ideal is precisely that it is unattainable. We may forever strive for it, but we can never reach it. 'Equality cannot be imagined outside of tyranny,' said Montalembert. It was, he said, 'nothing but the canonization of envy, [and it] was never anything but a mask which could not become reality without the abolition of all merit and virtue.'

"In the course of working toward equality, the state expands its power at the expense of other forms of human association, including the family itself. The obsession with equality, in short, undermines every indicator of health we might look for in a civilization. It involves a madness so complete that although it flirts with the destruction of the family, it never stops to consider whether this conclusion might mean the whole line of thought may have been deranged to begin with. It leads to the destruction of standards — scholarly, cultural, and behavioral. It is based on assertion rather than evidence, and it attempts to gain ground not through rational argument but by intimidating opponents into silence. There is nothing honorable or admirable about any aspect of the egalitarian program."

Leftists are calling Piketty's *Capital in the Twenty-First Century* "extraordinarily important," and "one of the watershed books in economic thinking." The resident radical at the *New York Times*, Paul Krugman, calls it "truly superb" and "awesome." Mr. Piketty wants to eliminate high incomes, wealth and what he calls family dynasties. He argues for an 80% tax rate on incomes over $500,000. He advocates an annual wealth tax of 10% on the assets of the rich and a one-time 20% tax on everybody's money. It's not so much that he wants to give it to the poor but to take it away from the affluent. To think that such a horrid prescription could resonate with liberals and cause them such joy tells you what we're up against in America.

In due time the left will have the votes to pull it off. The incredible number of people getting subsidies are a powerful voting bloc for the liberals. The poisoning of the minds of minorities and immigrants against what they believe to be social injustice adds more voters to the leftist cause.

Government-sponsored money creation and inflation is the primary cause of income inequality. It makes the wealthy people who own assets that much richer. Inflation shrinks the buying power of wages. The middle class can't keep up because their wage increases are less than the inflation rate. That's the consequence of misleading government statistics and lies about the extent of inflation. If you want to know the real rate of inflation, look backward to prices 10 or 20 years ago. Some experts suggest the real rate is 10%.

Mr. Piketty says he believes in free markets and entrepreneurship. However, his formula for eliminating income disparity would lead to poverty for all. Entrepreneurs would flee the country. Business would wither away and the economy crumble. The lights would go out in America. The current 50% tax rate already has the economy on the ropes. Sad to say as long as the left retains its influential positions in the media, the educational system and the government its 50-50 whether we will survive in any semblance of a free and prosperous nation.

CHAPTER 25

FOOD FOR THOUGHT

"If we can no longer control the government that is supposed to be serving us, we have lost something far more precious than money – our freedom."
Howard Ruff

Back in 1978, I began to get subscription offers in the mail from a guy in California named Howard Ruff. It seemed like every other day I'd get a mailing. He was pro gold and silver so I decided to give him a call. I got through to him right away and we had a nice conversation. However, he advised me that he had endorsed a coin dealer out east and was happy with that arrangement.

Two weeks later I got a call from a man that had done business with this company and was upset. He had wanted to buy gold coins but had wound up with a piece of paper. The coin dealer had put him into a highly leveraged margin purchase with exorbitant commissions and interest charges. He asked if I could help him.

I called Howard Ruff and told him that one of his new subscribers had been cheated by his recommended vendor.

Then I called the crooked coin dealer and brow beat him into giving the customer his money back. Then I had the customer let Howard know that I had helped him get a refund. Howard ditched his recommended dealer and I became the fair-haired boy for gold and silver. This was an enormous stroke of fortune for me.

Howard Ruff's newsletter took off like a rocket ship. His subscriber base grew over 125,000. His book became a runaway best seller and it recommended my company Investment Rarities. His newsletter never failed to mention us as a source for gold and silver. His seminars were packed with subscribers and my top salesman, Jesse Cornish, was a popular speaker at each one. We grew from two secretaries and myself in early 1978 to 300 employees in 1980. Our sales went from a few million to $525 million at the peak in 1980.

A few months after I got Howard's recommendation I traveled to California to meet him in person. Howard was a Mormon and one evening he took me to the local tabernacle where he gave a speech to young parishioners. He called it a "Fireside." His talk stressed

74

the importance of having a six-month supply of food on hand. Subsequently, I began to entertain the idea of acquiring a few cases of freeze-dried storage food. Eventually, I packed a big supply of this food in a corner of my basement.

Twenty-five years later I threw it all away. Months later my wife and I lugged home a number of large cases of storage food from Costco. Although we never used any of the first batch, we still decided to have more on hand. The likelihood of us ever having to rely on it seems remote. It's a form of insurance even though it's highly unlikely we'll ever have to dip into it.

A far more likely possibility exists for an unexpected financial event that disrupts the way we do things. I've always kept a good supply of silver coins on hand in case of hyperinflation. This was one of Howard Ruff's bedrock recommendations; keep a supply of silver coins at home in case the dollar loses its purchasing power. I don't think twice about adding silver, which I have done every year since 1981. It's not like storage food, which eventually spoils. It's permanent and it often appreciates.

Let's say the dollar goes kaput for a short time. Silver would be immediately recognized as a temporary money replacement. People would catch on to this value in exchange almost immediately. If cigarettes could serve as money as they did in Europe at the end of the Second World War, then silver would quickly fill the bill here. Other paper currencies, such as the Canadian dollar, might be used in exchange. Silver would quickly buy you a supply of this currency. A new U.S. dollar that replaced the defunct one would also be valued in gold and silver.

The mainstream media ridiculed Howard Ruff's survivalist aspects. So far, the warnings about runaway inflation have been wrong or premature. Nevertheless, if we knew such an event was certain, the hedges against it would be too expensive and if everybody anticipated it, it wouldn't happen. It's what we don't expect that gets us. Nobody, to speak of, expects a big, bad inflation. That makes it a more realistic possibility. For that reason a home supply of "survival silver" seems imperative. If you don't have a viable means of exchange in your possession during a currency crisis, you are vulnerable to misfortune. A lot of people laugh at such advice. I personally believe that a huge tidal wave of inflation is lurking somewhere offshore. That will be nothing to laugh about. If I'm right, silver coins and bars will save you.

CHAPTER 26

WHAT YOU SHOULD DO NOW

"The day will come when silver will be more valuable than gold as it was in Ancient Egypt."
Jerome F. Smith

My wife mentioned that a friend in her exercise class said that her husband was up all night worrying about a decline in his stocks. My advice to that fellow would be to put 20% of his portfolio into silver. We've tried to make the case that a lot can go wrong in our economy and our nation is on a slippery slope that can lead to an economic crisis. You absolutely need an asset that can preserve a percentage of your net worth in a financial collapse. We could see deflation or runaway inflation. World over the monetary authorities are committed to money and credit creation that knows no bounds.

When you are a gold and silver dealer, everything you write is suspect. People think you are not objective. In fact, when I read what other coin dealers write I often think it's self-serving. I'm in the precious metals business because of the way I think, not the other way around. In other words, I've stuck it out for 42 years through some mighty lean times (1987 to 1992) because I believe these metals are mandatory for the perilous period ahead and it will be a great investment and a good business.

The destruction of the dollar through runaway inflation does not mean the end of America. It just means if you hold paper and intangible assets, you will be ruined. The most liquid, divisible, portable and important assets you can own in an inflation are silver and gold. You can do things with these precious metals that you can't do with other assets. Once they are in your possession for a few years they become a hidden asset. Their demand rises during inflationary periods. Thus, they offset the ravages of a depreciating currency.

I believe that gold and most especially silver will increase the wealth of those who hold it. If renowned silver analyst

Theodore Butler is right, huge profits are coming in silver and at the very least you will make a lot of money holding silver. Theodore Butler is the world's foremost authority on silver (nobody else comes close) and he assures us that great profits lie ahead. Already he has impacted the silver market in so many ways and as more people become familiar with his work, silver becomes even more promising.

For one thing, the above ground supply of silver is perilously low. Around the time of the Second World War, the U.S. government held around 5 billion ounces of silver. That silver was entirely used up by industry and now the U.S. owns no silver. The U.S. mint has to acquire silver on the open market like any other user. The huge surpluses of silver that once existed are gone but the price of silver fails to reflect that fact. If any other commodity saw its historic level of inventory disappear the price would have skyrocketed and stayed at that record level.

Silver usage is said to be price insensitive. In other words, such small amounts of silver are used in each application a rise in price would not discourage its use. For example, an iPhone or iPad uses a tiny amount of silver. The price could go to $200 an ounce and it would not much affect the price of the phone. Substitutes for silver are few and far between. That's because the price has stayed so low nobody bothered to look very hard for a substitute. Theodore Butler claims that this is just one more reason for the silver price to explode. Industry has to have it, no matter what, because nothing else works as well.

Every year, hundreds of millions of ounces of silver are used up by industry and are gone forever. Very little silver is recovered as scrap. The low price and small amounts used in each product make recycling of silver marginally profitable. It used to be that photographic and x-ray film supplied a lot of reusable silver but those days are gone forever. The low price also virtually eliminates the melting of jewelry, silverware and coins. This greatly restricts recycling, an important source of supply.

A growing world population requires more silver. The spread of capitalism in Asia has increased demand for products that use silver. Everything electronic and electrical requires silver. Furthermore, you can hardly find a product that hasn't employed silver as a catalyst in its manufacture. Next to oil, silver is the most important ingredient in manufacturing the comforts and conveniences of modern life.

Meanwhile the supply of silver from mining faces a dramatic reduction. Low prices mean primary producers must curtail operations that are marginal or lose money. Exploration companies and small producers are already on the ropes. Permits for new mines face huge bureaucratic hurdles and regulations. Copper, lead and zinc mines that produce silver as a byproduct are under attack from environmentalists and low prices. All major mining companies are seeing a reduced level of new resources.

Theodore Butler predicts that all this will lead to a silver shortage. He sees evidence of a shortage in the millions of ounces of silver currently going in and out of COMEX warehouses, the major storage facility for silver bullion. The minute an industrial user can't get the silver they need on time, fear will grip the management of that company. For if they don't get the silver they need they will have to shut down their production. The natural reaction will be to buy more than they need. All the industrial users will begin to hoard silver. Silver prices will reach unheard of levels in this rush to buy silver.

When you superimpose investment buying of silver on top of heavy industrial use you have an additional wild card that can aggravate the shortage that Ted Butler predicts. When the fireworks from a shortage start, you have the biggest silver short position in history that must be bought back and covered. You have pool accounts and worldwide bank storage where no real silver exists that will have to be purchased. You will have everybody and his brother buying silver on a price rise, on top of an industrial users' buying panic, on top of a short-covering panic. If you own the real thing the screaming you hear for physical silver will be music to your ears. Theodore Butler has warned that all of this can happen in a hurry. It's imperative to own the silver beforehand.

It's true that silver has tried our patience over the past few years. Nevertheless, it still remains a superb value investment because in many cases it sells for less than the cost of mining it. That means you buy it and wait patiently for its true value to be recognized in the market. When that day comes, silver analyst Theodore Butler predicts there will be multiples of the current price. That means our patience will have paid off in a big way.

A GROWING WORLD POPULATION REQUIRES MORE SILVER. THE SPREAD OF CAPITALISM IN ASIA HAS INCREASED DEMAND FOR PRODUCTS THAT USE SILVER.

Not too many people know that banking giant JPMorgan has accumulated a huge stockpile of silver. They don't know there isn't a lot of silver above ground that's available for purchase. They are not aware that the billions of ounces that were once held by the U.S. have been used up by industry and are gone forever. They don't know that silver is a miraculous metal with so many important uses that it's grossly mispriced and severely undervalued. They haven't read Theodore Butler's missives that explain why a silver price explosion is the inevitable outcome of a price suppression.

At some point in 2011 when the price was high, JPMorgan must have realized the true dynamics of silver and opened their eyes to the enormous profit opportunity it offered. They have been accumulating silver ever since. Theodore Butler points out that JPMorgan has likely accumulated 400 million ounces of physical silver. Against that they have shorted 75 million ounces on paper. This isn't typical hedging as some would suggest. It's what Ted Butler insists is the mechanism to manipulate prices. The price of silver is set in daily trading on the COMEX futures market. By selling silver short, a big player can hold down the price. They can keep silver cheap while they hoard physical silver. However, all that needs to happen for the price to soar is for the big silver short to stop selling the paper contracts. Once that happens, it's off to the races.

The fact that JPMorgan owns so much silver virtually ensures that silver prices will climb. How much physical silver will the big bank want to own before they relax their short selling? This isn't going to go on forever. There are billions in profits waiting to be had by them. This train is going to leave the station and when it does, you want to be on board. It could be the ride of a lifetime. Hedge yourself against hard times with silver, and if silver analyst Theodore Butler is correct gain significant profit by owning this miraculous metal.

James R. Cook is the President of Investment Rarities Incorporated. He is the author of *The Start-Up Entrepreneur,* *The Great Gold Comeback,* *National Bankruptcy,* and the novel, *Full, Faith and Credit.*